GOODENOUGH
on
The History of Religion and on Judaism

Number 121
GOODENOUGH
on
The History of Religion and on Judaism
Edited by
Ernest S. Frerichs
and
Jacob Neusner

GOODENOUGH
on
The History of Religion and on Judaism

Edited by

Ernest S. Frerichs
and
Jacob Neusner

Scholars Press
Atlanta, Georgia

GOODENOUGH
on
The History of Religion and on Judaism

Edited by
Ernest S. Frerichs
and
Jacob Neusner

Library of Congress Cataloging in Publication Data

Goodenough, Erwin Ramsdell, 1893-1965.

Goodenough on the history of religion and on Judaism.

(Brown Judaic studies ; 121)
Includes index.
1. Judaism--History--Post-exilic period, 586 B.C.-210 A.D.
2. Jewish art and symbolism. 3. Philo, of Alexandria.
4. Religion--History--Study and teaching.
I. Neusner, Jacob, 1932-   . II. Frerichs, Ernest S. III. Title.
IV. Series.
BM176.G625   1986   296'.09   86-20320
ISBN 1-55540-062-0 (alk. paper)

Printed in the United States of America
on acid-free paper

For
Annette Boulay

Our Administrator
and
dear friend

With thanks
for her
devotion and loyalty,
wisdom and judgment.

CONTENTS

Preface

Writing about his *Jewish Symbols in the Greco-Roman Period,* Goodenough stated:

> I am bold enough to hope not only Judaism and the origin of Christianity may be illumined by the present undertaking, but I may also offer suggestions for a new methodology applicable to the whole spiritual history of the civilizations behind us...I have slowly been forced to suspect that the spiritual history of the development of Western man cannot be written as a set of disjunctive essays on the religion of each successive people and civilization, from Babylonia to the present. Rather it must be seen to be a continuous adaptation of certain basic symbols.
>
> These volumes are then submitted ultimately as a contribution to a field in which no one is as yet an expert. That field is symbolism in the most general and contemporary sense.

So Goodenough explains his purpose in the study of Jewish symbols in particular. Indeed, as we see, his vision encompassed the whole of human spiritual history. That explains Goodenough's greatness, why he deserves a hearing for a long time to come. Because, along with his teacher, George Foot Moore, Erwin Ramsdell Goodenough was the greatest historian of religion produced in America, his work retains abiding interest. Since his greatest contributions concerned, in particular, the study of the history of Judaism in late antiquity, we have chosen to make available to a new age some of the papers he himself regarded as important and of lasting value. In this way we aim to secure for Goodenough that hearing in the twenty-first century that, in our judgment, he has amply earned for himself.

Erwin Ramsdell Goodenough was born in Brooklyn, New York, raised in a theologically conservative Methodist family, studied at Hamilton College, Drew Theological Seminary, and Garrett Biblical Institute, from which he received his bachelor's degree in theology in 1917. He then spent three years studying at Harvard with George Foot Moore, the first important historian of religion in America, and another three years at Oxford. He received his D. Phil. from Oxford in 1923, and in the same year became instructor in history at Yale University. He spent his entire career at Yale, being named Professor of the History of Religion in 1934 and John A. Hoober Professor of Religion in 1959. He retired in 1962 and spent a post-retirement year teaching at Brandeis

University. The complete bibliography of his writings, by A. Thomas Kraabel, appears in J. Neusner, ed., *Religions in Antiquity. Essays in Memory of Erwin Ramsdell Goodenough* (Leiden, 1968: E. J. Brill), pp. 621-632.

Goodenough deserves the fresh reading made possible here and in the forthcoming abridgement of his *Jewish Symbols in the Greco-Roman Period* (Princeton, 1986: Princeton University Press, ed. by Jacob Neusner) as well as the reprinted editions of his *Introduction to Philo-Judaeus* (with an introduction by Jacob Neusner) (Lanham, 1986: University Press of America *Brown Classics in Judaica*) and his *Psychology of Religious Experience* (with an introduction by William Scott Green) (Lanham, 1986: University Press of America *Brown Classics in Judaica*) for a simple reason. It is that through his studies of earliest Christianity and Judaism he not only attained the rank of premier American historian of religion of the twentieth century but also provided the model for how future work should go forward. That is a status achieved, among native Americans, only by George Foot Moore. Along with Moore's *Judaism* and Goodenough's *Jewish Symbols*, moreover, no other single work has so decisively defined the problem of how to study religion in general, and, by way of example, Judaism in particular. Goodenough worked on archaeological and artistic evidence, so took as his task the description of Judaism out of its symbolic system and vocabulary. Moore worked on literary evidence, so determined to describe Judaism as a systematic theological structure. Between the two of them they placed the systematic study of Judaism in the forefront of the academic study of religion and dictated the future of the history of religion in the West. It would encompass not only the religions of non-literate and unfamiliar peoples, but also of literate and very familiar ones. In all, Moore and Goodenough have left a legacy of remarkable power and intellectual weight. Through the study of Judaism they showed how to describe, analyze, and interpret religious systems, contexts and contents alike.

It follows that Goodenough's importance nearly a quarter century after his death derives from two facts. First of all, much of his work remains seminal and exemplary. People have still to consult it when studying topics on which he worked – and they are able to learn something fresh and suggestive. Second, we are entering a period in which the approach to the study of religion represented by history of religion is enjoying enormous attention, as scholars experiment with other-than-theological modes of describing and interpreting religions and religion. Goodenough provides a model for a new generation of scholars.

This volume provides the definitive picture of Goodenough on the study of religion, with special emphasis upon Judaism. The opening section reviews his most rigorous efforts at the definition of what we do when we study religion, his definition of history of religion. We turn then to Judaism as studied in important, specific ways by Goodenough. The papers we have selected were those he himself designated as "important." They moreover retain substantial scholarly value today, serving not merely as chapters of a now-concluded past but as valued positions of contemporary interest. No volume of his essays exists, and the one we have put together covers everything one would include – and nothing one would exclude – in a permanent and enduring record of scholarly exploration and achievement. A companion volume on the history of Christianity is planned.

Goodenough spent much of his life working on Jewish art and symbolism. In a separate volume, we present an abbreviation of his great work, *Jewish Symbols in the Greco-Roman Period* (Princeton, 1986: Princeton University Press). In his reading of these symbols, we meet Goodenough's basic notion of Philo's Judaism, for he interprets the symbols by reference to Philo's writings and proposes to describe a mystical, Greek-speaking Judaism, represented by both Philo and the artists who decorated the ancient synagogues. We see in this book how Goodenough debated a different reading of Philo. By simply reviewing the finds, Goodenough forced the scholarly world to reconsider its consensus and to come to a thoughtful reappraisal of its earlier position. Goodenough's essential contribution is to be measured by evaluating not his "proof" of any of this theses, but rather his method and its *cumulative* consequences. Goodenough forced some of us to take seriously the question posed by the Jewish symbolic vocabulary yielded by ancient synagogues and sarcophagi. With reference to both Philo and synagogue art Goodenough does not claim to "prove" anything, for if by proof one means certain and final establishment of a fact, there can be no proof in the context of evidence such as this.

At the period between the first and sixth centuries, the manifestations of the Jewish religion were varied and complex, far more varied, indeed, than the extant Talmudic literature would have led us to believe. Besides the groups known from this literature, we have evidence that "there were widespread groups of loyal Jews who built synagogues and buried their dead in a manner strikingly different from that which the men represented by extant literature would have probably approved, and, in a manner motivated by myths older than those held by these men." The content of these myths may never be known with any great precision, but comprehended a Hellenistic-Jewish mystic mythology far closer to the Qabbalah than to Talmudic Judaism. In a fairly limited time before the advent of Islam, these groups dissolved. This is the plain sense of the evidence brought by Goodenough, not a summary in any sense of his discoveries, hypotheses, suggestions, or reconstruction of the evidence into an historical statement.

Because *Jewish Symbols in the Greco-Roman Period* covered twelve volumes of text and pictures as well as a thirteenth volume of index, few readers worked their way through the whole. The price was reasonable, but only specialists read the whole. Consequently, the work reached its audience principally through the reports of reviewers. While not all of the reviews proved hopelessly unsympathetic and supercilious, enough of them did so that

Goodenough's achievement scarcely registered in his own day. Reviewers who, after he died, purported to lay down the verdict of history proved only their high regard for their own opinions, with the result that, twenty years after Goodenough's death, his work has lost access to that large world of literate and interested readers, interested in symbolism and the definition and meaning of religion, that Goodenough proposed to address. Goodenough deserves a general audience, because, through the specific case of the symbolism of ancient Judaism and problems in its interpretation, he raises a pressing general question. It is how to make sense of the ways in which people use art to express their deepest yearnings. And how are we to make sense of that art in the study of the people who speak, without resort to words, through it.

The importance of Goodenough's work lies in his power to make the particular into something exemplary and suggestive, to show that, in detail, we confront the whole of human experience in some critical aspect. Goodenough asks when a symbol is symbolic. He wants to know how visual symbols speak beyond words and despite words. We find ourselves surrounded by messages that reach us without words, that speak to and even for us beyond verbal explanation. Goodenough studied ancient Jewish symbols because he wanted to explain how that happens and what we learn about the human imagination from the power of symbols to express things words cannot or do not convey. It is difficult to point to a more engaging and critical problem in the study of humanity than the one Goodenough took for himself. That is why, twenty years after the conclusion of his research, a new generation will find fresh and important the research and reflection of this extraordinary man.

In 1963 Goodenough asked me what I thought he had contributed. I turned the question on him and now report his answer: What do you think? I recall my surprise at how he understated his contribution. Goodenough was a great man, one of the few truly great human beings I have known in scholarship. The modesty of his assessment of his own work strikes me as evidence of that fact. At the same time, let it now be said that he had a sense of not having been adequately appreciated in his day. Even when he lay dying, Goodenough expressed a sense of disappointment and hurt. Academic life sometimes turns paranoia into understatement. But Goodenough's continuing influence, the keen interest in his work two decades after his death, surely vindicates him and marks him as one of the giants of his age.

Goodenough does not claim to "prove" anything, for if by proof one means certain and final establishment of a fact, there can be no proof in the context of evidence such as this. The stones are silent; Goodenough has tried to listen to what they say. He reports what he understands about them, attempting to accomplish what the evidence as it now stands permits; the gradual accumulation of likely and recurrent explanations derived from systematic study of a mass of evidence, and the growing awareness that these explanations point to a highly probably conclusion. That is not a "demonstration" in the sense that a geometrical proposition can be demonstrated, and for good reason are the strictly literal (and, therefore, philological) scholars uncomfortable at Goodenough's results. But all who have worked as historians even with literary evidence must share Goodenough's underlying assumption, that nothing in the endeavor to recover historical truth is in the end truly demonstrable or positive, but nonetheless significant statements about history may be made.

Goodenough would claim that he has clearly indicated in his words, "a substantial probability recurrently emerging from this mass of evidence." If the cumulative evidence is inspected as cautiously as possible, it can hardly yield a statement other than the following: At the period between the first and sixth centuries, the manifestations of the Jewish religion were varied and complex, far more varied, indeed, than the extant Talmudic literature would have led us to believe. His judgment on the use of symbols in synagogue art bears review, since the essays here cannot be understood except as part of the broader thesis they help spell out and articulate:

> At the end these symbols appear to indicate a type of Judaism in which, as in Philonic Judaism, the basic elements of "mystery" were superimposed upon Jewish legalism. The Judaism of the rabbis has always offered essentially a path through this present life the father's code of instructions as to how we may please him while we are alive. To this, the symbols seem to say, was now added from the mystery religions, or from Gnosticism, the burning desire to leave this life altogether, to renounce the flesh and go into the richness of divine existence, to appropriate God's life to oneself.
>
> These ideas have as little place in normative, rabbinic Judaism as do the pictures and symbols and gods that Jews borrowed to suggest them ... That such ideas were borrowed by Jews was no surprise to me after years of studying Philo.

What is perplexing is the problem of how Jews fitted such conceptions into, or harmonized them with, the teachings of the Bible.

Pagan symbols used in Jewish contexts include the bull, lion, tree, crown, various rosettes and other wheels (demonstrably not used in paganism for purely decorative purposes), masks, the gorgoneum, cupids, birds, sheep, hares, shells, cornucopias, centaurs, psychopomps, and astronomical symbols. Of the collection, Goodenough writes (VIII, p. 220):

> They have all turned into life symbols, and could have been, as I believe they were, interpreted in a great many ways. For those who believed in immortality they could point to immortality, give man specific hopes. To those who found the larger life in a mysticism that looked, through death, to a final dissolution of the individual into the All ... these symbols could have given great power and a vivid sense of appropriation ... The invasion of pagan symbols into either Judaism or Christianity

... involved a modification of the original faith but by no means its abandonment.

Symbolism is itself a language, and affected the original faith much as does adopting a new language in which to express its tenets. Both Christians and Jews in these years read their Scriptures, and prayed in words that had been consecrated to pagan deities. The very idea of a God, discussion of the values of the Christian or Jewish God, could be conveyed only by using the old pagan theos; salvation by the word soteria; immortality by athanasia. The eagle, the crown, the zodiac, and the like spoke just as direct, just as complicated a language. The Christian or Jew had by no means the same conception of heaven or immortality as the pagan, but all had enough in common to make the same symbols, as well as the same words, expressive and meaningful. Yet the words and the symbols borrowed did bring in something new ...

Goodenough continues (VIII, p. 224): "When Jews adopted the same lingua franca of symbols they must ... have taken over the constant values in the symbols."

Goodenough's argument is that literary traditions would not have led us to expect any such art as such has turned up in the ancient synagogues. We may find statements in Talmudic literature which are relevant to the art, but we must in any case after assembling the material determine:

what this art means in itself, before we begin to apply to it as proof texts any possible unrelated statements of the Bible or the Talmud. That these artifacts are unrelated to proof texts is a statement which one can no more make at the outset than one can begin with the assumption of most of my predecessors that if the symbols had meaning for Jews, that meaning must be found by correlating them with Talmudic and biblical phrases [IV, 10].

One may continually say that the use of pagan art is wholly conventional, just as the critics of Goodenough's earlier interpretations repeat that the symbols from graves and synagogues were "mere ornament" and imply nothing more than a desire to decorate. But having asserted that pagan art has lost its value and become, in a Jewish setting, wholly conventional, we have hardly solved many problems. For by saying that the "art has lost its value," we hardly have explained *why* pagan conventions were useful for decoration. Goodenough holds that these were not participants in the "established traditions of Judaism," and that they did not have close contact with Babylonian or Palestinian Judaism.

No account of Goodenough's monumental work can ignore the critical debate that he precipitated. Anyone with an interest in symbolism will follow that debate as a first step beyond this encounter with Goodenough's work. A mark of the success of scholarship, particularly in a massive exercise of interpretation such as the one at hand, derives from how a scholar has defined issues. Did Goodenough succeed in framing the program of inquiry? Indeed he did. Nearly all critics concede the premise of his work, which, when he began, provoked intense controversy. So the judgment of time vindicated Goodenough in his principal point. Goodenough demanded that the Jewish symbols be taken seriously, not dismissed as mere decoration. That view formed the foundation of his work, and he completely succeeded in making that point stick. Few today propose to ignore what, when Goodenough began work, many preferred to explain away. So Goodenough's greatness begins in his power to reframe the issues of his chosen field. In his day few scholars in his area enjoyed equivalent influence, and, in our day, none.

But that fact should not obscure differences of opinion, both in detail and in general conclusions. Goodenough would not have wanted matters any other way. Readers will find useful an account of two interesting approaches to the criticism of Goodenough's *Jewish Symbols*, as well as a list of the more important reviews of his work. These readings will pave the way to further study not only of Goodenough alone, but also of symbolism and, by way of example, of the symbolism of Judaism.

In *Gnomon* 27, 1955, 29, 1957, and 32, 1960, Arthur Darby Nock presented a systematic critique of Goodenough, Vols. 1-8, under the title, "Religious Symbols and Symbolism." Now reprinted in Zeph Stewart, ed., *Arthur Darby Nock. Essays on Religion and the Ancient World* (Oxford, 1972: Clarendon), II, pp. 877-918, Nock first summarizes the main lines of Goodenough's approach to the interpretation of symbols. He then expresses his agreement with what I regard as the principal result of Goodenough's work for the study of Judaism (pp. 880-82, *pass.*):

> G[oodenough] has made a good case against any strong central control of Judaism: it was a congregational religion and the local group or, in a large city such as Rome, any given local group seems to have been largely free to follow its own preferences. Again, in art as in other things, Judaism seems to have been now more and now less sensitive on questions of what was permissible. From time to time there was a stiffening and then a relaxing: down into modern times mysticism and enthusiasm have been recurrent phenomena; so has the "vertical path" as distinct from the "horizontal path." To speak even more generally, from the earliest times known to us there has been a persistent quality of religious lyricism breaking out now here, now there among the Jews....

The point conceded by Nock is central to Goodenough's thesis: that Judaism yielded diversity and not uniformity. Again, since Goodenough repeatedly turns to Philo for explanation of symbols, it is important to see that Nock concedes how Philo may represent a world beyond himself:

> So again, in all probability, Philo's attitude was not unique and, deeply personal as was the warmth of his piety and his sense of religious experience, we need not credit him with much original thinking. The

ideas which he used did not disappear from Judaism after 70 or even after 135. Typological and allegorical interpretation of the Old Testament continued to be common. G.'s discussion of the sacrifice of Isaac is particularly instructive; so are his remarks on the fixity and ubiquity of some of the Jewish symbols and (4.145 ff.) on lulab and ethrog in relation to the feast of Tabernacles, "the culminating festival of the year" with all that it suggested to religious imagination.

Menorah, lulab, ethrog, Ark and incense-shovel were associated with the Temple and as such could remain emblems of religious and national devotion after its destruction; the details of the old observances were discussed with passionate zeal for centuries after their disuse. G. has indeed made a strong case for the view that, as presented in art, they refer to the contemporary worship of the synagogue (as he has produced serious arguments for some use of incense in this). It may well be that they suggested both Temple and synagogue.

But Nock provided extensive and important criticism, of Goodenough's ideas. He expresses his reservations on detail (pp. 882-83):

The improbability of many of G.'s suggestions on points of detail does not affect his main theses, but those theses do themselves call for very substantial reservations. Thus the analogy between Isis and Sophia is more superficial than real, and so is that between allegorical explanations of the two types of religious vestments used by Egyptians and the two used by the High Priest. No these are not minor matters; the first is one of the foundations of what is said about the "saving female principle" and the second is made to support the supposition of Lesser and Greater Mysteries of Judaism.

The crucial question is: was there a widespread and long continuing Judaism such as G. infers, with something in the nature of a mystery worship? Before we attack this we may consider (a) certain iconographic features regarded by G. as Hellenistic symbols – in particular Victories with crowns, Seasons, the Sun, and the zodiac; (b) the cup, the vine and other motifs which G. thinks Dionysiac; (c) the architectural features which he interprets as consecratory.

The important point to observe is how Nock calls into question not only detail but the general approach: the main results. That is how scholarly debate should go forward. But Nock concludes (p. 918):

Once more such points do not destroy the essential value of the work. I have tried to indicate. . . what seem to be the major gains for knowledge which it brings and naturally there are also valuable details.

In the balance, Nock's systematic critique confirms Goodenough's standing as the scholar to insist that the symbols matter. More than that Goodenough could not have asked. More than that Nock did not concede.

Morton Smith's "Goodenough's Jewish Symbols in Retrospect" (*Journal of Biblical Literature* 1967, 86:53-68, and note also Goodenough, Vol. 13, pp. 229-30) provides the definitive account of his own viewpoint on Goodenough's work. Smith first calls attention to the insistence on distinguishing the value of a symbol from its verbal explanation (p. 55):

> The fundamental point in Goodenough's argument is his concept of the "value" of a symbol as distinct from the "interpretation." He defined the "value" as "simply emotional impact." But he also equated "value" with "meaning" and discovered as the "meaning" of his symbols a complex mystical theology. Now certain shapes may be subconsciously associated with certain objects or, like certain colors, may appeal particularly to persons of certain temperaments. This sort of symbolism may be rooted in human physiology and almost unchanging. But such "values" as these do not carry the theological implications Goodenough discovered.

The premise of a psychic unity of humanity, on which Goodenough's insistence on the distinction at hand must rest, certainly awaits more adequate demonstration. Smith proceeds (pp. 55-56):

> After this definition of "value," the next step in Goodenough's argument is the claim that each symbol always has one and the same "value."
>
> Goodenough's position can be defended only by making the one constant value something so deep in the subconscious and so ambivalent as to be compatible with contradictory "interpretations." In that event it will also be compatible with both mystical and legalistic religion. In that event the essential argument, that the use of these symbols necessarily indicates a mystical religion, is not valid.

So much for the basic theory of symbolism. Smith proceeds (p. 57) to the specific symbolism at hand:

> The lingua franca of Greco-Roman symbolism, predominantly Dionysiac, expressed hope for salvation by participation in the life of a deity which gave itself to be eaten in a sacramental meal. This oversimplifies Goodenough's interpretations of pagan symbolism; he recognized variety which cannot be discussed here for lack of space. But his these was his main concern, and drew objections from several reviewers, notably from Nock, who was the one most familiar with the classical material.
>
> It must be admitted that Goodenough's support of this contention was utterly inadequate. What had to be established was a probability that the symbols, as *commonly* used in the Roman empire, expressed this hope of salvation by communion. If they did not *commonly* do so *at this time*, then one cannot conclude that the Jews, who at this time took them over, had a similar hope. But Goodenough only picked out a scattering of examples in which the symbols could plausibly be given the significance his thesis required; he passed over the bulk of the Greco-

Roman material and barely mentioned a few of the examples in which the same symbols were said, by those who used them, to have other significance. These latter examples, he declared, represented superficial "interpretations" of the symbols, while the uses which agreed with his theory expressed the symbols' permanent "values." The facts of the matter, however, were stated by Nock: "Sacramental sacrifice is attested only for Dionysus and even in his cult this hardly remained a living conception;" there is no substantial evidence that the worshipers of Dionysus commonly thought they received "his divine nature in the cup." So much for the significance of the lingua franca of Greco-Roman Dionysiac symbolism.

Smith then points out that Goodenough "ruled out the inscriptional and literary evidence which did not agree with his theories." He maintains that Goodenough substituted his own intuition, quoting the following: "The study of these symbols has brought out their value for my own psyche. . . ." By contrast, Smith concurs with Goodenough's insistence on the hope for the future life as a principal theme of the symbols.

Still, Smith maintains that Goodenough failed "to demonstrate the prevalence of a belief in sacramental salvation" (p. 58). In Smith's view, therefore, "the main structure of his argument was ruined." Smith makes a long sequence of *ad hominem* points about Goodenough's background, upbringing, religious beliefs, and the like, e.g., "He is the rebellious son of G. F. Moore" (p. 65). In this way he treats scholarship as an expression of personal idiosyncracy, for instance, background and upbringing, dismissing Goodenough's learning. He leaves in the form of questions a series of, to him "self-evident," claims against Goodenough's views. These claims in their form as rhetorical questions Smith regards as unanswerable and beyond all argument. For example: "But the difficulties in the supposition of a *widespread, uniform* mystical Judaism are formidable [italics Smith's]. How did it happen that such a system and practice disappeared without leaving a trace in either Jewish or Christian polemics? We may therefore turn from the main argument to incidental questions" (p. 59). Those three sentences constitute Smith's stated reason for dismissing Goodenough's principal positions and turning to minor matters. Goodenough, for his part, had worked out the answers to these questions, which he recognized on his own. Still Smith's criticism cannot be dismissed, nor should we wish to ignore his positive assessment (p. 61):

Goodenough's supposition that the Jews gave their own interpretations to the symbols they borrowed is plausible and has been commonly accepted. His reconstructions of their interpretations, however, being based on Philo, drew objections that Philo was an upper-class intellectual whose interpretations were undreamt of by the average Jew. These, however, missed Goodenough's claim: Philo was merely one example of mystical Judaism, of which other examples, from other social and intellectual classes, were attested by the monuments. For this reason also, objections that Goodenough misinterpreted Philo on particular points did not seriously damage his argument; it was sufficient for him to show that Philo used expressions suggestive of a mystical and sacramental interpretation of Jewish stories and ceremonies. The monuments could then show analogous developments independent of Philo. Some did, but most did not.

The single most important comment of Smith is as follows (p. 65):

> Goodenough's theory falsifies the situation by substituting a single, anti-rabbinic, mystical Judaism for the enormous variety of personal, doctrinal, political, and cultural divergencies which the rabbinic and other evidence reveals, and by supposing a sharp division between rabbinic and anti-rabbinic Judaism, whereas actually there seems to have been a confused gradation.

Declaring Goodenough to have failed, Smith concludes (p. 66): "Columbus failed too. But his failure revealed a new world, and so did Goodenough's." For more than that no scholar can hope. For learning is a progressive, an on-going process, an active verb in the continuing, present tense.

Rereading Goodenough after two or three decades reminds us that he began much but concluded nothing. That marks the measure of his greatness. Obviously, this brief account serves only to call attention to the magisterial work at hand. Goodenough wanted nothing more than to insist that the art matters and that Philo remains interesting and worth reading. That is why he wrote: to bring a new generation once more to ask the old questions. People may or may not come up with Goodenough's answers, but they will have to work along lines dictated by his premises and follow his methods, whole or in part. He was the greatest historian of religion of his generation, and, as premier scholar, he cared not so much for conclusions as for process, not so much for scoring points as for the reasoned conduct of argument and inquiry. He leaves the legacy not only of learning but also of a great life, lived for illumination.

Jacob Neusner
For both editors

Program in Judaic Studies
Brown University
Providence, Rhode Island

Acknowledgements

The editors express thanks to the following copyright holders for permission to reprint the articles in this volume, as follows:

"Religionswissenschaft"
   Religion Ponders Science, ed. E. P. Booth (New York, 1964: Appleton-Century-Crofts Inc.), 63-84 © 1964

A Historian of Religion Tries to Define Religion
   Zygon 1967, 2:7-22 © 1967

The Bible as Product of the Ancient World
   Five Essays on the Bible. Papers Read at the 1960 Meeting of the American Council of Learned Societies (New York, 1960: American Council of Learned Societies), 1-19 © 1960

Literal Mystery in Hellenistic Judaism
   Quantulacumque: Studies Presented to Kirsopp Lake by Pupils, Colleagues, and Friends, ed. R. P. Casey, S. Lake, and A. K. Lake (London,1937), 227-241 © 1937

Philo's Exposition of the Law and his *De vita Mosis*
   Harvard Theological Review 1933, 27:109-125 © 1933

Wolfson's *Philo*
   Journal of Biblical Literature 1948, 67: 87-109 © 1948

Jewish Symbolism
   Encyclopaedia Judaica (Jerusalem, 1971), 15:568-578 © 1971 by Keter Publishing Co.

The Evaluation of Symbols Recurrent in Time, as Illustrated in Judaism
   Eranos-Jahrbuch 1951, 20:285-319 © 1952

The Rabbis and Jewish Art in the Greco-Roman Period
   Hebrew Union College Annual 1961, 32:269-279 © 1961: Hebrew Union College-Jewish Institute of Religion.

Part One

HISTORY OF RELIGION

Chapter One

"Religionswissenschaft"

Religion Ponders Science, ed. E.P. Booth
(New York, 1964: Appleton-Century-Crofts, Inc.), 63-84

Some essays must begin with a footnote, and the German title of this one certainly demands explanation. I have used the German word because no English term means what I shall be discussing. *Religionswissenschaft* means the scientific study of religion, but not in the modern English sense of the term, for those who "count and measure" have arrogated "science" to themselves, and of course religion cannot be approached on any important level by controlled experiments or differential equations. The German word still means the medieval *scientia,* that is, critical, ordered, analytical study, and it is of scientific study of religion in this sense that I am writing.

Our contemporaries in all directions urge upon us the futility of *Religionswissenschaft.* During the last twenty-five years especially we have been hearing how science, philosophy, and religion move on different levels of knowledge, and that through revelation we go beyond the whole scientific method, because science must draw its conclusions from analyses of material data. The religious man's intellectual problem, on the contrary, it is argued, is essentially to comprehend the depths and implications of revealed truth. To people who thus divide their ways of thinking, any attempt at a science of religion runs into absurdity, is a basic contradiction of terms. For it is to treat the holy, the numinous, the religious, as though it were a matter for profane scrutiny. Nearly a century ago the great Canon Sanday of Oxford, torn between the new analytical temper and his own devout faith in Anglican Christianity, cried out in agony, "We kill in order to dissect." The agony has since then proved too much for many of our most sensitive spirits. Perhaps they will practice science, do so brilliantly, so long as they can keep up the wall of utter contrast between the sacred and the profane, and do their science in such fields as not to impinge on what they call sacred. But the science of religion is meaningless unless we see that it essentially breaks this down, and proposes precisely in the realm of the religious to move from empirical data to hypothesis, and from hypothesis back to data, and to correct hypotheses by data, as nearly as possible in scientific fashion. It will have no meaning unless we do so with the data of all religions, with the data of the religion we were early taught to love quite as fully as with the religions of Asia, Central Africa, or Australia.

Hereby, it seems, we may perhaps see why study of the history of religion, or of *Religionswissenschaft,* has now generally declined, and has never gained any recognized place among the departments of American universities at all. A century ago, those who felt most torn in Europe were the men who, like Sanday, applied the new methods of historical criticism to the Bible. American scholars went to Europe during the last half of the nineteenth century, and learned the methods of European criticism, and brought back the German solution of Ritschl and Harnack, that the *Wesen* of Christianity is its social and ethical teaching, a facile solution that Schweitzer very effectively exploded at its roots. Almost simultaneously the Papal Bull of 1912 rejected all such analytical methods for Catholics, and I cannot see how the Pope could have made any other decision. For the analytical study of the sources of Christianity did indeed break down the old distinctions between the sacred and the profane. What had to be God's Word for the Church, for Protestants, really as well as Catholics, had in the hands of historians become a collection of historical documents from which history was to be gleaned by only the most rigorously detached scrutiny. I recall Kirsopp Lake's saying once to a graduate class, "The genuineness of a saying attributed to Jesus can be judged only by men free if necessary to say without emotion that, so far as they can see, Jesus did teach in the way under discussion, but that on this point they disagreed with Jesus." The historian might reject or accept the saying attributed to Jesus as authentic, but not on personal or ecclesiastical grounds. From the point of view of the historian, Lake was absolutely right: we cannot let our own or our Church's ideas or preferences interfere consciously or unconsciously with our decisions as to what Jesus did or did not teach. But the Pope was right in saying that such an attitude does indeed break down the safeguards of the sacred as the Christian has to conceive it if the Church is to continue at all in its traditional way.

Meanwhile in the nineteenth and twentieth centuries, men studied the myths and rituals of the world with increasing detachment. The relative merits of Max Müeller's school of cosmic origin, Durkheim's social-totemistic origin, Taylor's animism, and Marett's mana, with a variety of other suggestions, could be debated with complete freedom in a secular world whose leaders largely thought in the new channels of a boundlessly optimistic evolutionism. The crudity of man's roots only emphasized the beauty and value of the emergent tree, the civilization of William II of Germany, Edward VII of England, and William Howard Taft of America. For many devout people revelation became progressive revelation, and scholars delighted in tracing the evolution from the crude Yahweh of the Book of Judges to the Christian God, who, finally, could "love" but not "desire." Frazer became a household word. Anthropologists concerned themselves largely with gathering material on the religions of the world. The new scientific criticism invaded the four leading American centers of religious study, the divinity schools of Harvard, Yale, Union, and Chicago. No one who heard them will ever forget the great lectures on the history of religion given by George Foot Moore.

America's special contribution to the analysis of religion, however, was made by our psychologists. While all the leaders of thinking in the history of religion were Europeans or Englishmen, and Americans were eagerly reading their books, all Europe and England were reading William James, Starbuck, Leuba, and Pratt. These men had a new and startling view of the roots of religion, roots not in a past perhaps a hundred millennia comfortably removed, but in our own immediate and personal psyches. Religious individualism of America had split the social organization of religion into a hundred controverting fragments, and Americans regarded religion as a private matter in which the state should never interfere except to protect individuals and minorities. Through practically inventing new approaches to the psychology of religion, this American spirit made its idiomatic contribution to the scientific study of religion, a contribution that Europeans with their state churches did not attempt to rival. You will all object, perhaps, that Schleiermacher, Herbert Spencer, and Louis Sabatier had followers when they, each in his own way, proposed a more individual and psychological approach. But Europe and England generally agreed with Durkheim at least in his minimizing such movements, and defining religion as a unified system of beliefs and practices relative to sacred things, which bring their adherents into a single moral community called the Church. Even so great an individualist as Freud all his life saw in religion a block of entrenched beliefs and practices which he had to fight in order to protect the individualistic approach of his own psychology. He thought he was fighting religion, when, as it seems to me, he was founding and practicing one of his own.

Since the series of collapses that followed upon the catastrophe of 1914, the scientific study of religion has fallen off rapidly. Depression took hold of the defeated Germans of 1918, and in this condition their religious leaders, succumbing to the magic of Karl Barth, regarded the scientific approach to anything whatever as the great sin of men, who only made fools of themselves when they supposed that by taking thought they could add to their stature. Christian revelation, the new-old theology said, had taught man the complete sovereignty of God, the pusillanimity of man, and the sacrilege of supposing that man's critical study of anything, religion least of all, could hope to improve man's essential way of life. Two new words for the profane became widely current, namely science and history, and Barth and his followers would fain lead men not only out of the damning preoccupation of their study, but altogether out of the world these words imply, lead men to a world in which they find their existence in a metaphysical reality.

The great financial depression of the late twenties and thirties made such an escape from the world of science and history deeply attractive also to frightened and discouraged men and women of England, France, and America. With the horrors of the Hitlerian war, more and more people, from different points of view, came to accept the new emphasis upon the inherent sinfulness of man and the mockery of his analytical and scientific efforts. Science makes instruments only to destroy us, people cry out in terror, and to them this demonstrates the inherently depraved nature of science, a doctrine, incidentally, they are not above broadcasting by the latest scientific gadgets. The modern age is re-enacting the tragedy of all Greek drama, they say, the tragedy that the gods inevitably bring destruction upon men who in *hubris* try to do the superhuman. One of the leaders of this sort of thinking loves to describe how God rocks in derision on his throne at the spectacle of man's trying by science to help himself, to improve himself in what this preacher calls the world of history. Man's only hope is in a divine act of revelation. The contents of this revelation we can examine, formulate, assimilate, but the critical attitude of science has no relevance to it. I recently listened to a discussion of the bearing of psychology, both experimental and depth psychology, on theology. Clearly most of those in the room considered that the criteria for examining ordinary psychological experiences had no relevance to man's experience of God and revelations. Science was very well in its place, but as a man-made thing it was futile, hopeless, and entirely impious if it invaded the field of religion.

Theological schools and religious leaders now largely preach variations in this message of human futility. In spite of a scattered remnant, it is precisely *Religionswissenschaft* in any meaningful sense that the religious leaders of our generation have rejected. Are we ourselves ready to face the world as a group prepared and eager to modify our operating hypotheses, which in religion means our faiths, if scrutiny of empirical data makes them dubious or suggests better ones?

The remnant of historians of religion with scientific attitude is now largely scattered in a wide variety of fields: linguistics, anthropology, area studies, sociology, and the like. Leaders in these fields have in large part accepted the old definitions of religion, by which such scholars are not only classed as irreligious by most contemporary religious leaders, but are delighted to find themselves thus described, and call themselves irreligious. Scholars in these fields, consequently, have in general turned their attention to other things than what they consider religion. Most anthropologists now have only tangential interest in religious phenomena. Not by chance did anthropologists study religions avidly a century ago, and now study social structure. Religion was the burning issue then. Now social structure, by the rise of Communism, the threats of the dictatorships, and the problems of industrial relations, stands at the forefront of all our minds. We must not fool ourselves: our scholarship reflects our own basic problems, and the modern intelligentsia feel these social problems much more intensely than the problem of the sacred and the profane.

The same change has occurred in psychology, which has largely tried to become scientific by asking only questions that can be answered by counting and measuring. The psyche as a whole lies quite beyond such control, and so at times modern psychology seems almost obsessed with what one might call psychophobia. One cannot set up problems of the sacred and profane in a rat maze and one does not try to do so. Consequently, I know no really important book on the psychology of religion published in the last thirty-five years. Psychologists who work in personality testing have not tried to develop tests that would show sensitivity to the sacred and profane. We have tests of aptitude for almost everything except for reverence of the "sacred."

The great psychologists that have come out of psychoanalysis have divided sharply on this point. Freud, as I said, tried to brush away the whole matter by showing that the illusion of creedal religion was doomed to collapse before such a deeper understanding of man as he was offering. We may well doubt that Freudianism, as it was systematized by his orthodox followers, is any less illusory as a final statement of the nature of man than the statements Freud characterized as illusions; but Freud provokes us to ask whether authoritatively drawn distinctions between the sacred and the profane, what Freud accepted as being religion from the religious experts of his day, really constitute religion, and whether their acceptance basically marks the *homo religiosus*. Jung went further when he put his whole psychology upon a religious basis by proposing that all individuals have their foundation in the collective unconscious. This conception we might well call mana in direct action, or the panpsychism that has haunted Western thinking from Aristotle to Hegel, and which really underlies Buddhism and Hinduism. I am not a Jungian, but we must admit that Jung has done more than any one man of our generation to keep from utter neglect the problems that worldwide similarities in religious experience thrust before us. I must digress a moment to record that among the great experiences of my own life, not generally know, were the hours in 1938 that Jung spent in my own study (not I in his as a patient), when the already huge mass of my material on symbols threatened to overwhelm me, and when, to use his term, I was trying to "integrate" it all by, as always, integrating myself. Like the great therapist he was, he helped me largely by encouraging me to help myself, not by telling me how I should regard the material. There was healing in his wings. But Jung, let us face it, has generally been rejected by our generation, those who call themselves religious and those who call themselves irreligious, and behind rejection of such a brilliant way of thinking must lie a reason. The reason, if in one reason I may summarize the many, is that somehow he has not spoken the word this generation wants to hear. To his ideas, however, we shall keep recurring, not only in this paper, but in all our studies.

This generation wants either an assurance that its true existence is not in the scientific world, or it wants analytical precision. So *Religionswissenschaft* has suffered from the new and specialized sciences, which, in their highly proper craving for precision, have taken science away from religious studies. Linguistic science, for example, has captivated most of the best minds that have gone into Sinology, Indology, and Islamic studies. Or documentary history, and precision in textual editing, now dominate the minds of young men who came into our departments with quite other objectives. The professors have felt that generalizations about the *Religiosität* of the documents might well await accurate texts and genuine *Sprachgefühl*. Who could assail such impeccable and impregnable correctness? Who but those of us still interested in *Religiosität*, since we find ourselves deserted not only by the new theology, but also by those who through their technical skills could help us most? In these departments a remnant of the old interest survives in many people, who still read the religious classics with deep perception of their religious as well as linguistic or literary value. The greatest scientists of our day, however, are by no means denouncing religion. They have little in common, as I know them, with the theologians who demand that scientists keep within their province of carding wool so that the theologians can weave their cloths. The best scientists I know are deeply devout persons who see the numinous through their telescopes or microscopes, and in their test tubes, not in an "other," but as the essential quality of matter, matter as exploding atoms, or galaxies, or as biological processes.

The hope of reviving study of the science of religion lies, I believe, not in courting the traditionalists and theologians, but in coming to recognize that science itself is a religious exercise, a new religion, and that science and religion have fallen apart largely because traditionalists have done what they have always done, failed to recognize a new approach to religion as it has formed itself in their midst, challenging thereby old conceptions and comfortably formulated adjustments. Historians – of religions, that is – must include in their study, and in their sympathy, the new religion of science, or of scientists, along with the religions and thought ways they have hitherto considered. This needs a bit more explaining.

For the term *science of religion* to have any meaning, we must obviously return to ask what we mean by *religion,* since by the old definitions the two are essentially in contrast. I have no illusion that I shall do more than make suggestions for the problem.

As a historian rather than a philosopher, I must say that no definition of religion I have ever heard, or made (and I have made many), has any but suggestive and partial value. The most important words, of course, can never be defined, and deeper understanding of them usually involves discovering the inadequacy of old definitions. Even so precise a term as chemistry can no longer be defined. What, today, is it? Who will now sharply distinguish it from physics or botany? Certainly not the students of chemistry themselves. Nuclear physics can be studied apart from chemistry, or biology, or astronomy, to a point, but only to a point. *A fortiori,* who can set up any but pretty verbal barriers between history, science, and philosophy? Similarly Freudians have come to understand sex better as they have confused the rest of us by seeing its manifestations everywhere, even in the conduct of infants. Man is a physiological animal, a sexual animal, a political animal, an economic animal, a social animal. He is also a religious animal. He is all of these simultaneously, for beneath the distinctive terms is man himself. Those who study man from one point of view rather than another always tend to see their own approach as the one really all-encompassing in human structure. The function and goal of *Religionswissenschaft* is to come better to understand the *homo religiosus*. But all these approaches blend so inextricably that to define the character and compass of any one aspect invades the boundaries of every other. If we do not recognize this, we limit to the point of petty distortion that aspect we try to define. Sociologists and psychologists have no notion of defining their fields in such a way as to exclude the other, or, in fact, of excluding man's religious patterns. Religion, in turn, cannot be forced to define itself in such a way as not to impinge upon, indeed largely to include, at least sociology and psychology. So, if we are not by verbal calisthenics to weaken our understanding of all these fields, we must resort to description that moves from an essential center indefinitely outward, rather than fabricate definitions that work from borders inward.

In brief, then, I see religion arising from the universal phenomenon that we are born and live in an external universe, and with internal depth and emotions, which we neither understand nor control. Man exists largely helpless before the forces of nature and society, and really knows nothing basic about himself, and the meaning and purpose of life, individually or collectively. The conscious mind, and probably even more persistently the unconscious mind, are always confronted by the *tremendum,* both within oneself and without. By modern science man has to a slight degree mitigated the sense of helplessness and confusion he feels before the *tremendum,* but now when men collectively know more than ever in history, we call ourselves the Age of Anxiety, because we are freshly, almost pathologically, sensitive to the ignorance and helplessness that characterize us. Such ignorance has always characterized mankind, characterizes all animal life. But if an animal is hungry, while he looks eagerly for food, so far as we know he has no diffused anxiety about the problem of food supply. Or of death, or sex, or security in general. Without debating whether that be true for mice and rabbits, or for rats that have been psychologically tortured, this generalization will stand better than most, that awareness of our helplessness and ignorance, along with the anxiety they produce, generally characterizes human beings.

Religion steps in for all of us at this point. Man has never been able to accept himself on this level as helpless before the *tremendum.* He must have the illusion, at least, that he can do something to control the apparently uncontrollable, to explain the inexplicable. We may laugh at the savage stories of creation through the cosmic bull, or turtle, or egg, but the understanding most people have of the process of evolution is probably just about as far from reality, and starts from quite as vague a protozoan, or protozoa, as the stories of the savages. It gives us comfort, nevertheless, to believe in evolution. Those least satisfied by the theory of evolution are my friends in biology who know how fragmentary and inadequate the whole theory really is. All great tragedy faces the unintelligibility of life, and terrifies us as it suddenly dangles our helpless ignorance before us. Shakespeare had no answers for Hamlet and Lear. The *Oresteia* loses its dignity when Athena at the end introduces a divine justice that exists in religion, not reality. For Aeschylus had finally to succumb to his craving for divine consolation, and so he projected its reality as Socrates did not. But how few men in history have given their lives rather than deny their own ignorance! For one such man there have been untold millions of Athenian citizens who would murder, and not always mercifully by hemlock, a man who doubted the reality of the myths that they held like curtains to screen themselves from the unintelligibility and uncontrollability of the *tremendum*.

Here seems the essence of religion, the problem of how man can live over against the great unknown, the *tremendum*. Traditional religions have given two basic answers. Most commonly man has screened himself off from the *tremendum* by mythical accounts of the origin and nature of things, by rites that would placate its unpredictable lightnings and whirlwinds, by holy places and seasons, by divinely given codes of laws. In all these ways man has tried to protect himself from what is to him the chaos of the *tremendum*. Man has draped curtains about him, with fine paintings in perspective on them. This perspective could give him the illusion that he lives in the *tremendum* itself while the curtains actually only protect him from its impact. The patterns on other people's curtains are, of course, myths; those on our own are theology. The masses of men must get their myths, their rites, and their codes, their symbols, the designs on their curtains, from the traditions of their social groups. Few can escape them, or make new ones of their own. Since a few can do so, however, our myths of explanation and our rites for controlling nature, or fate, cannot be simply social institutions forced upon all. And those of us who break away are not thereby irreligious, else the Jewish prophets, the Buddha, Socrates, and Jesus were irreligious.

As over against the apotropaic, the second basic formulation is that in which an individual has broken the curtains, or lifted them, to go alone into the Alone, and to face the numinous *tremendum* in itself. Moses on Sinai, the prophets announcing their new visions, Jesus at Gethsemane, the Buddha as he left his earthly kingdom, many young savage candidates to achieve spiritual leadership in the tribe, these represent an utterly different conception of an adjustment to the universal reality from which most men screen themselves. These men left, or still leave, the formulation about them, to court the very *tremendum* itself, and be taken over by it. Buddhist monks practice this approach, and train the more intelligent laymen in it, though it has little appeal to the mass of Buddhists who live almost entirely in their apotropaic exercises.

The history of religions examines this drive of man to adjust himself to the *tremendum*, the masses by screening themselves from it, others by freshly approaching it. About the *tremendum* itself as a whole, we all come out with myths, of course, whether with traditional myths or ones of our own creation, since the *tremendum* as a whole is utterly too much for us. Practical living is impossible without a skeleton of myths that establish values and meaning. The myths of men have given them their courage both to live and love, and to destroy and kill. It is in the name of myths proclaiming a meaning of life that Hitler and Lenin killed, and Gandhi refused to kill. All decisive action, in the last analysis all action and life, comes from faith, pure faith that the nature of the *tremendum* is thus, and so, and so, and that we have such or such relation to it. If true religion be a matter of formal revelation from the *tremendum*, however, those who assert that science and its methods have no relation to it cannot be disputed. In that case, study of the history of religion would be to collect curious information about behavioral aberrations and strange myths, essentially not religious at all, because not a part of what we consider revelation. Its members might have much good information, and practical advice to give diplomats or businessmen in dealing with peoples of the world, but their work would have no relation to *Religionswissenschaft*. Perhaps we should assume, on the other hand, in Jungian terms, that religion is a matter of less formal, but no less real, invasion of humanity by the *tremendum* through the emergence of universally similar rites and myths. In that case, by accepting the Jungian hypothesis that these materials come to man through the Collective Unconscious, we can perhaps get increasing insights into the nature of the *tremendum*. But, to be brutal, this approach may well be only another method for obscuring from ourselves our ultimate ignorance, and of painting new designs, or a new term, on our curtains. Whether we think this fair to Jungians or not, most scientists would at once say that the Jungian approach goes too rapidly from data to overall conclusions.

Can a really objective approach to the value of the myths and practices of religions ever be found? Is one myth painted on the curtain as good as any other? Should we believe anything that makes living and dying comfortable, and destroy those who would shake our belief and so disturb our comfort? As one Catholic wrote me: "There are too many things we shall never know. Here it seems to me is the role of the revealed religions, of which there is only one true one, meaning mine, for the simple reason that Catholicism did it so much better than any other religion." This is, indeed, the usual pattern of religion, especially in the West, including modern Russia with its Gospel according to Marx. At this point the science of religion, with the history of religions as one of its chief tools, can step in. For we shall believe that only our cowardice makes the *tremendum* terrible, and that so long as we admit our ignorance we can step up to the *tremendum* itself in matters of human value as physics does in matters of material value (if we can use the word *material* any more). The method of modern science is, unabashed by general ignorance of reality, to go to the great unknown with little questions that inch their way into bits, consistent bits, of knowledge. I believe that in the science of religion we must learn to do the same.

Personally, I do not see how in the modern world we have a right to speak of, or look for, a science of religion so long as we ourselves live within apotropaic curtains, or live with the stated purpose of having our personalities and critical faculties blurred out in mysticism. For we can no longer use the world *science* in its original sense of the Latin *scientia,* or of Plato's *episteme.* Science now means, as I have said, a method of study in which, by the most exact methods applicable to a given sort of data, we draw up hypotheses from the data, and then verify (or reject) the hypotheses by some fresh return to the data, or by return to fresh data. A cataloguing of data, or a learned collection of information, can no longer pose as scientific knowledge, what the world *Wissenschaft* often meant a century ago. Scientific study takes empirical data and tries to see the principles inherent in them. Science proverbially says it can do nothing with an isolated fact. It can do just as little with inherently miscellaneous facts. For what science seeks always is structural, inherent relationships.

In saying this about science we seem to have begun again describing religion, since religion has been man's passionate attempt to adjust himself to the *tremendum* by understanding its nature and how to use it. It is possible that the rejection of science by religion, and of theology by science, is only the old war of religions on a new front, and that science seems a threat to old formulations of religion precisely because it is a new formulation of man's relation to the *tremendum,* actually a totally new form of religion itself. I believe that that is precisely the case and that the emergence of this type of thinking, which followers of the old religions continue to mark as irreligious, signifies the emergence of a new religion. The new religion takes a new attitude toward the *tremendum:* It no longer hides its head, ostrich-fashion, in myths asserting that the *tremendum* is less perilous than it is; it no longer surrenders to the *tremendum,* and asks to be reabsorbed into it. Instead, refusing either to run away or to surrender, it accepts the *tremendum,* and the individual's helplessness and insignificance before it. It drops no curtain, but faces the overwhelming within and without, while it seeks to find relationships and meaning as far as it can by its own method. The new religion of science, and most of the men and women who practice it, have few illusions. Few of them want to discuss the nature of reality, or work from *a prioris,* except the basic one announced by Einstein, that the only thing unintelligible about the universe is that it should be intelligible. To assert that the universe is universally intelligible would indeed be another painted curtain. Certainly it is not intelligible now. But society finds itself deluged with the apparently limitless flow of dimes from the jackpot of nature that the scientific conception of intelligibility has released upon us. As Theodore Sizer remarked the other day, the new deluge, in the eyes of millions, has been enormously rewarding but depressingly stupefying. In other words, science has released not only gadgets and dimes to engulf us, but has stupefied us with the *tremendum* itself, and that in a way for which we have formed no protective devices. It has often stupefied even the scientists in their private lives, but does not do so in the lives of those truly dedicated to the new point of view, people whom I may call the saints of science. Many of them have a private logion, such as that of the great astronomer Harlow Shapley, who, as he looks in his telescope, or does his celestial mathematics, mutters to himself: "All nature is God, all God is nature." He approaches this nature-God, however, not by traditional forms of worship, but through his observations and calculations, which have become his sacrament. Few human beings have a conception of the immensity of the universe, or of the smallness of man in it, comparable to Shapley's. But the *tremendum* has no terror for him. He looks at it with quiet eyes, astonished, reverent, but unafraid. He carried this attitude over to society and politics when McCarthy created fear and trembling. He regarded Senatorial Committees for Hysteria with the same calm eyes, and spoke up to them as, in his mathematics, he speaks up to the universe. Throughout he keeps his integrity, his dignity, as an ignorant but seeking human being. This is religion pure and undefiled, and we do ourselves, and our subject, small service if we fail to recognize it as such.

Much of this spirit must become ours. For we can hardly call ourselves scientists of religion if we systematically define religion so as to leave out this great approach to the *tremendum* going on all about us, and refuse ourselves to share it. In the mid-twentieth century we will seem ridiculous to our generation if we call ourselves scientists but do not examine our data in the same factual and calm spirit. We cannot announce the nature of the *tremendum,* but must content ourselves with shuttling back and forth between data and hypotheses, happy when one of our hypotheses proves useful, but quite undismayed and willing to discard them when others do not. For our faith, like that of all scientists, will be that the process will eventually advance us to sounder understanding, not that our hypotheses of the moment have ultimate validity.

In such study our audience will be small. We shall have little that will seem valuable to the great mass of men who live within the curtains of a revelation or within the far narrower and uglier curtains of indifferent and insensitive preoccupations, which are the local and private blinders of much of our modern society.

And what, exactly, will be our data?

For *Religionswissenschaft* in general the data will be of many kinds. No field of human activity, really, can be thought irrelevant. We may get most important suggestions from the study of psychology of all sorts, from all sociological studies, including, of course, anthropology and law. Increasingly the new linguistics, whether as a study of the structure of language, the more accurate approaches to etymology, or the whole new philosophy of semantics, will help us. The worlds of creativity in art, literature, and music are worlds of religion. No one person can deal with such diversified data. Many particularly concern themselves with the sacred literatures and ethics, as well as the myths and rituals, of people of the world from earliest times to the present. Insofar as our study of this is scientific, it will involve detailed analyses conducted with full awareness of the best understanding others have achieved from such data up to the point of our own investigation. It is not, if we are analyzing Pahlavi texts from Iran and India, that we will know merely all former suggestions for the meaning of those particular texts, but that we shall know similar analyses elsewhere, so that our work will add at once to the understanding of the particular texts, and also to the general technique of textual analysis. This brings us one step nearer the *tremendum,* since the phenomenology of textual transmission has broad horizons. If analysis of our particular data takes us into strange fields, we go out into them. It is a common experience that one analyzing texts in one language will find cognate texts in another language, so that he must stop and learn the other language. It may be that a scientific study of rabbinical law is going to require knowledge of Greek and Roman law, or, for the Babylonian Talmud, of the laws of Babylonia. In that case the obligation before the scholar is clear. There are limits to this, the limits of human capacity and length of life. We often must publish, using data beyond our expert competence. Such publication must not only state the limits of the author, but be written by an author who will always bear in mind that what he writes is beyond his expert control.

Herein we can never fulfill the ideals of a natural scientist, who can so control his observations that they involve no extraneous variables. But at this point I hear the chuckles from my scientific friends. Of course that is the ideal, they say, but just what experiment of any but routine importance was ever done in any science when all variables were controlled? Scientists try to recognize those variables, and take them into account, they tell me, but the advance of science has largely meant that the next person discovers variables that had not been suspected at all. The *tremendum* again.

We can hope to re-establish a science of religion not insofar as we take over too slavishly the various methods now used in other sciences. Scientists have to invent new methods for appraising each new type of data. Science has only one method, and that is to devise in each case and for each body of data or for each question a method, usually quite *ad hoc,* which will yield the most adequate understanding of that data. But the questions scientists ask of their data are relatively small ones. Science advances only bit by bit, and most scientists regard the questions of philosophy as quite outside their proper realm, indeed as *hubris* when they invade science itself.

Scientists, however, can never lose sight of the fact that the particular problem is always part of a larger problem, for only in that relation lies scientific creativity. We hope to clarify the larger problem by solving the smaller, but in simply solving the smaller we are technicians and antiquarians, not people adding to scientific knowledge at all. The great prophets of science, or the great historians, have been masters of their techniques (though in this they have often had research assistants who could correct them sharply), yet they have been supreme because they have gone beyond the techniques of what I may call the pharisees of science. Creative scientists, like creative painters and musicians, advance into the *tremendum* as they try methods never used, join the hitherto unconnected, break all rules as they seem inadequate, even though earlier men had found those rules useful. Science, like religion, has been led and fed by men who have used their micrometers, but looked beyond them. For the spark of new light always is an understanding of the data that the data themselves do not give to those whose eyes focus too narrowly upon them.

In studying the data of man's religious history, we, too, must look beyond the data. But not too fast. We must look how and for what? Look by the most detailed study for a spark of new light on man as a *homo religiosus*. A young geologist remarked to me the other day that the modern scientist works always confronted by the vastness of unknown nature. But he does not drop his tools to generalize about it. He works on his own specific problem. Our specific problems will be somewhat analogous to those who investigate native herbal medicaments to see if they can find their value (many had great value), and so get suggestions of new drugs for our own use. Somewhat similarly we would ask: What actually lies behind the values men have found in myths, mystic philosophies and practices, rituals, and symbols? As historians of religion this will be our specific field of investigation. Before we can do any valuable generalization, we must do a great deal of careful, detailed study of local phenomena. We must beware of the occupational disease of people in our fields, which is to make such generalizations about religious phenomena as were made by the great leaders in *Religionswissenschaft* of the last century. The old method, still by no means abandoned, was to assume we are proving such generalization if we can give examples of cases where we think they apply. It is almost impossible not to fall into this error if we make too large generalizations too soon. In fields where evidence is hopelessly inadequate, we must work with hypotheses supported only by a few instances. But in those cases we work fully aware of the hypothetical nature of our conclusions, as a biologist must do in discussing the stages of evolution. At the present stage of the science of religion, we would do well to ask small questions until we have established a methodology we can all approve and use.

Such a procedure does not mean that we will ever lose sight of our true objective, total understanding. But we must face the *tremendum qua tremendum*, not reject old curtains only to put up new curtains of hasty generalizations.

Most of us will be technicians, turning up carefully verified hypotheses about small and isolated problems. We also will have our reward. Always, however, we shall hope that new Curies and Einsteins will come in our field to use what we have been doing, and go far beyond it into a new dimension. The *tremendum* about us and within us will still have *n* dimensions. *Religionswissenschaft* in the mid-twentieth century can take us not to total understanding (perish the *hubris*), but to somewhat greater comprehension of man in his religious problem. It can do so only as we combine science and religion in our very marrow, combine them into a dedication to learning about religion by the slow, dogged approach of science. I know no other way in which we can hope eventually to understand better the *homo religiosus*, religion itself, and avoid the agony Sunday felt when he killed in order to dissect. For if we still have to kill the old dream that religion is a matter of revelation, through *Religionswissenschaft* we may discover that the scalpel itself has become a sacramental instrument.

That is, we must learn this much, at least, from psychoanalysis, that we cannot understand other people until we understand ourselves. In calling the myths and theologies of religions painted curtains, designs so drawn in perspective that one forgets the flat canvas on which they are painted, I have, of course, only partially described the function and value of traditional religions. To change the figure, the projections of men have often been dream ropes they have thrown up into the *tremendum,* and then have miraculously been able to climb them a little. All human development has taken place as men have dreamed, for example, of social justice, and then spent the millennia from the beginnings of tribal justice to hopes of the One World in climbing that rope. All who have understanding of religion know that much of great value has been painted on men's curtains, that mankind has actually climbed on those ropes. We know also that much that was hideously destructive has been taught in the same of religion. The great new hope, I believe, is in *Religionswissenschaft* itself, which proposes minutely to examine the *homo religiosus,* including ourselves as *homines religiosi,* quite aware that overall and hasty generalizations only curtain us off again from our subject. We should use the curtainless procedures of science, whose essential temper was oddly best expressed by that curtain-bound genius, Cardinal Newman, when, although hating free inquiry of any sort, he wrote:

> I do not ask to see the distant shore:
> One step enough for me.

Religionswissenschaft writes no popular books, no simplified summaries for sophomores. Perhaps we must make our living doing this, but we must recognize in it no part of our real business, for the soul of the new age sees human existence as the endless road of inquiry. Science offers no royal road to knowledge, but an unblazed trail into the wilderness, where, if we travel with understanding, we travel with awareness of its vastness, but move from tree to tree.

So we shall take to ourselves the advice of the ancient rabbi: "He who grasps much, grasps nothing; he who grasps little, really grasps."

Chapter Two

A Historian of Religion Tries to Define Religion

Zygon 1967, 2:7-22

A paper on love, loyalty, or justice would gain little by pedantry by starting out with a concise definition of the term. Only as we describe the various conflicting elements associated with such words could we finally arrive at a resultant meaning within their complexities. In important matters we understand not as we simplify but as we can tolerate and include. Each important aspect of our lives overlaps every other. Even an apparently distinct feature like childhood runs into our maturity, so that no adult can be understood apart from the child still living in him. A colleague of mine told me he had once tried to define poetry in such a way that his formula would include all the kinds of literature to which the word had been applied. When he had finished, he said, his definition had become so broad that no one had any use for it. I strongly suspect, however, that in making so universal a definition he had come to an understanding of poetry much richer and deeper, even if less clear and specific, than that of those with more limited statements. For clarity is often won at the expense of depth of understanding.

Religion presents an outstanding example of this difficulty. Those who think they know most clearly, for approval or disapproval, what religion "is" seem to recognize least what amazingly different aspects of life the term has legitimately indicated. We can, therefore, best approach religion by getting in mind the various experiences that men have called religion, rather than what we think ideally should be given the name.

A man is commonly considered religious or not according as he assents to, belongs to, follows the practices of an organized religious faith. When we speak of the religions of the world we are ordinarily taken to refer to Christianity, Judaism, Islam, Buddhism, and the like. "Primitive religions," those traditionally practiced in the Pacific Islands and central Africa or by the Australian aborigines, seem to most people to be rather incipient, nascent religions than religions in any acceptable sense. In lectures on religion such phenomena are usually discussed under the "origins of religion," as contrasted with expositions of the "world's great religions." For the religious practices of savages are shot so full of what many call "magic, superstition, and idolatry" as to seem not to have reached the level of "religion" at all. Even William James did not include religion on this level among his "varieties" of religious experiences. Here I need only point out that little as we may approve the religious ideas and practices of savages we can hardly deny that these constitute their religions. Metaphysicians and theologians usually distinguish between what seem to them aberrations in religion, which they do not like to call religion, and real religion, which is their own ideal formulation.

A person who has studied anthropology or the history of religion must take another path, for he knows how great a variety of objects of devotion men have had. We cannot define religion by saying that it is the worship of God or the gods, but we can define God or the gods by saying they are whatever is the object of devotion. Jesus pointed this out clearly when he said that we cannot worship both God and money, or mammon. Here Jesus as usual was being visionary, since men have always worshiped the security money brings, and always will, but have combined it with love of others (to a point), and even with worship of the God of idealized existence. Sometimes devotion to one's business and social position so takes over that one becomes almost a monotheistic worshiper of mammon, though many mammon worshipers like to belong to stylish churches. Most of us just plug along in polytheistic devotion to science, money, metaphysical dreams, family, social success, and what not.

Sources of Security

Religion is this devotion, dedication, and tremendous concern for and with the sources of security. Religion for most of us is a very immediate concern, as when the Groton boys almost all take communion the Sunday before examination week. Tillich's Ultimate Concern does not make them do this, but terror at the coming ordeal, and hope that there is something, somewhere, that will help them through it. The common element in all religions, that is, religion itself, seems to be a devotion to something on which the people committed seem to themselves to depend, or in which they hope for security, or in which they seem to themselves actually to find it. Whether it is the security given by a fetish, by a ritual, by the loving Jesus, by one's social status, by a substantial bank account, by a title (whether the title be president of the bank, professor, or marquis), or by creativity in art or science, in each of these forms of religion the common element is a focusing of life upon one or more of them as a source of security.

Man lives now, as he has always lived, in a universe, in a human society, and in the face of inner conflicts, all of which threaten to engulf him, and some of which sooner or later will do so. In helplessness people of all civilizations begin their lives, and in helplessness all end them. Although as adults we can somewhat fend for ourselves, all the deeper experiences of personal life and the exigencies of society emphasize the essential importance of the individual. The mass of men in Canada and the United States, in western Europe and England, live in a security that other men have rarely known. That we make even of this an "Age of Anxiety" shows how inescapably man feels the uncertainty of life. During the "Golden Age" of the nineteenth century, as nostalgic cowards now often conceive it, life expectancy was just half that of our day; pain expectancy, physical torture, cold in winter, inescapable heat in summer, these sat with every man at his fireside and table. With this for the greater part of mankind everywhere went social insecurity, recurrent famine, devastation by arms and invaders. It would be ridiculous to say that we now live in complete security. I only say that even with our relatively far greater security man does not feel more secure, because he has more time to reflect, to pity himself for his still essential helplessness, and to write and read about it. In the "death urge" Freud indicated an amazing aspect of human nature; for he showed that the urge to kill, which at one time we turned against animals and one another, we now turn inwardly upon ourselves. Not only does nature give us ample grounds for anxiety, but man demands anxiety, creates it within himself, when nature and other men for a time seem to let him alone. What we used to call the "balance of power" we now call a "cold war," so far as I can see only to torture ourselves. Since man alone among animals, apparently, has the power to anticipate coming agonies and death, man is inherently an anxious animal, ever crossing fancied bridges of terror when no actual threats immediately confront him.

I call these threats, or sense of them, collectively the *tremendum,* a Latin word that Otto used in a somewhat different sense and that has, as I use it, its simple original meaning of "that which must be feared" or "the source of terror." I use it precisely because its strange vagueness best conveys the most terrifying part of man's predicament, the very inchoateness of the terror outside and within him.

Human beings as a whole have never been able to face the *tremendum* as such. Two ineluctable necessities have always forced themselves upon man: one, he must feel that in some measure he understands himself, his origin, his natural environment, and his destiny; and, two, he must give himself the illusion that he has some little control over things. There must be something he can do about it all. Insofar as man has the second illusion, that he can control the uncontrollable, he loses his sense of futility and helplessness. The drive for control has not only produced the gadgets of civilization; it has expressed itself in religious practices of all sorts, from what higher civilizations call "magic," to the ritualistic acts and prayers of the church or the political party, or to the private rituals we all consciously or unconsciously observe. This begins with the earliest childhood: thumb-sucking, the fetishistic blanket, familiar routine in familiar surroundings, sleep ritual, these the child early demands. He may give up some, but as he does so he will cling to others all the more earnestly. Man's rituals make the individual participate in the *tremendum* to a slight extent, at least, and give him a feeling that by these acts he appeases the *tremendum* or makes it more apt to befriend him. By the rituals, also, he keeps himself from consciously facing the *tremendum's* unfathomable depth and power, the actual abyss of the uncontrollable. We all invent little rituals, but few individuals have been able to invent enough to satisfy themselves. In childhood the mother or nurse supplies them to the child. She keeps the child always near her or puts him in a playpen where a fine little world is nicely boxed in for him and the universe excluded. An eighteen-month child is far happier in such a pen than alone in a five-acre lot. Still happier are the little ones strapped to the mothers' backs. In later years the church or other conventions of society give him other rituals to perform, prayers to say, amulets to wear. Conventional dress is a ritual. We would all be as uncomfortable at a ball in the sport clothing worn here as we would be here in the clothing of a ballroom. As ladies lived in a world where men tipped their hats and gave them seats on a trolley car they lived in a world that was safe. And oddly enough it had the same effect on the men. The drive to security by joining in the procession of the seasons, if only the gay flowers and ribbons in our straw hats in spring, and with the return to felt hats in the fall, produced the great religious festivals; and our concept of a moral law of nature solidified the great legalistic aspects of religion to which we shall return. Rituals of healing, ablution, burial, puberty – these are all manifestations of religion's giving man security from the *tremendum* by an illusion that he is controlling it.

But witch doctors do cure the sick, as do practitioners of faith healing. When the psychoanalysts say they cannot help a patient until his "resistance" breaks down, I suspect they have only invented a new term for an old phenomenon, since they too can do their work only in an atmosphere of faith.

The magic of faith: is it religion or magic? The question has reduced itself to tautology. Faith that we can do the superhuman, like killing or healing another person by suggestion, gives us power to do the superhuman. Through faith we do control the uncontrollable, some of it, a little. Those who have "lost their faith" often speak of the loss as though they had lost sight or hearing, a faculty of some sort that made them able to do things to themselves and for themselves which now they cannot do. They are quite right; they have lost a real potency, a real power of control. So I must say that to call a belief a "superstition," a ritual "magic," only pronounces a value judgment or a feeling of taste. These are religious beliefs and acts which the person calling them superstition or magic simply does not like.

Before leaving this part of our subject, however, we must ask how the religious attempts to control differ from man's ingenuity in inventing devices by which he indeed gives himself superhuman power, devices that range from the stone implement that multiples his striking force to the airplane, atom bomb, and computer. At the end we shall suggest that concern with expanding knowledge and control can themselves become a religion for scientists, but, in general, control through understanding the forces of nature stands in sharp contrast to traditional religion, which has been an attempt to control without such understanding. If a Tyrolean peasant protects his house by building a shrine for the Virgin into its walls, we call it religion, but not when men in the western prairies, with their terrible thunderstorms, protect their houses by putting lightning rods upon them. But our new powers of control have by no means checked inevitable invasions of the uncontrollable *tremendum.* I cannot assert that men will never be able entirely to control nature for their own ends, but I can say that adequate control does not now appear remotely possible. Such control would do away with man's need of religion, but we need not seriously discuss that eventuality.

Explanation of Beliefs

I have just referred to the second universal in man's religious pattern by speaking of man's "beliefs." By this I do not mean his control through scientific knowledge but the creeds, myths, and philosophical and theological systems by which he gives himself the illusion that he understands the *tremendum* outside and within him. Perhaps some day we shall know better, but as far as we can now see man alone among the animals has this craving to understand. Some people, of course, have the craving more than others, but all people of normal intelligence must have a sense that they understand nature and their place in it or that their leaders or priests do so. In ancient days, and still among savages, the authorities were usually the "old men." These created stories or, more usually, passed on ones they had once heard from their elders in an indefinite succession of old men – stories of creation, of the origin of evil and the necessity for work, of the stars, the heavens, the depths of the sea, of the origin of life and death, of male and female, good and evil, and of life after death. Such stories the old men told in personal form, as though in answer to questions of four-year-old children: "Who made the world; where is grandma who died; who makes the thunder; who blows the wind; who paints the grass green; who makes the waves in the sea?" The answers we give our children are often apt to be personal also, in terms of God the creator, but in primitive times all the answers were centered in persons, so that all nature became populous with personalities, some of them greater and more powerful than man, but in most respects quite like him. Other such "persons" had the spooky character of the forms men meet in dreams – phantoms, yet with human personalities and motives. The advance of science has put physical forces such as gravity or electric power in the place of most of these personalities, but non-scientific civilizations still account for the storms and plagues as manifestations of the wrath of divine persons much as Homer did. Insanity and illness are seen as demonic possession. Man can face the perils of life so much better if he feels that he understands, or that the medicine man does so. If Christianity, and still more science, has since given us different sorts of answers from this, the primitive still persists in our reactions to the horrible, such as the birth of a mongoloid. A Person must have done this to us. And the idea has formal legal confirmation in what the law describes as "acts of God," that is, all disasters from natural causes such as storms or floods.

We ordinarily call "mythology" the attempt to explain nature in terms of such personalities and their activities. But if we now define "myth" as an explanation of reality given to conceal from ourselves our lack of understanding, then myths are with us in all aspects of modern life. Like most people I am not a natural scientist, and so the scientific accounts as I finally understand them, and the implications I draw of how the forces of nature operate, are all ridiculously mythological from the point of view of real science. I am neither a vitalist nor a non-vitalist because scientists themselves do not agree on the subject, but I am ready to go either way when they decide upon a theory, whether I myself understand it or not. Meanwhile, of course, I live in a mythical world in which "dead" and "alive" are absolute opposites, and I find for my purposes that that myth serves very well. I use my pseudo-scientific myths of nature for two reasons: first, to have a rough and ready understanding with which I can meet the problems of life and, second, to have a sense that I am not lost in a meaningless *tremendum*. Ancient myths and creeds served all these purposes.

Individuals have rarely dared to face the fact that they live in an unknown world, about them and within, and no society has tried to face it. "Agnosticism" is an unpopular word, and "agnostics" are suspected individuals because they challenge the pretense of men's beliefs and throw men back upon the ignorance and helplessness, which, by their myths and rituals, they are trying to conceal from their own horrified eyes. To live in full awareness of their ignorance would crush the vast majority of human spirits. So between themselves and the incomprehensible they have universally put curtains painted with explanations, to give themselves the illusion that they understand the meaning, nature, and destiny of themselves and the world about them. To these explanations, along with rituals of control, every other element in religion is secondary. Scholars of religion have taken as its basis various notions, such as "mana" and the "idea of the holy," as contrasted with the profane. But none of them proves to be universal, and each has been challenged by other scholars. Each is too specific, and in religion the basis and the primary solutions are not specific at all. The common element is the quite vague insecurity and diffused anxiety, which different peoples and different individuals experience and meet in different ways. Only the insecurity and the craving for an explanation and control remain universal, along with every civilizations' projecting primitive or sophisticated myths, rites, creeds, and faiths to make painted curtains about them. The vast majority of men get these curtains and their ready-made designs from their societies, whether from dogmas given by stated organizations of a professional religious group, or from the "old men" or "old women" of the tribe, or, often today, from journalistic reports of college courses that introduce us to the fringes of scientific theory and give us, like other myths, the illusion of understanding. Religion accepts such accounts as truth, not hypothesis, and makes men pattern their lives on them. Not the truth of the account but its acceptance and one's commitment to it constitute religion. True or false, the stories and rituals become religion when they are accepted as describing our universe, the reality in which we live, and when they actually make the unformed *tremendum* seem something formed and manageable.

Fear and Love

Thus far I have described religion as man's devices for escape from fear into peace of mind. If the fear of the Lord, or of the *tremendum,* is not the beginning of wisdom in our sense, it has universally been thought of as the beginning of religion. Those sects of Christianity flourish best which most emphasize the terrors of purgatory and hell. Traditional Protestantism and Catholicism alike have gone on to mitigate the terrors they have first evoked – or given concrete form to. The sacred always implied punishment for its violation. So holy images, objects, even holy words, and forms, cannot be used lightly or "in vain," for they have an inherent power to punish misuse, or a power behind them will punish. "I, Yahweh, am a jealous God, visiting the iniquity of the fathers upon the children to the third and fourth generation" (Deut. 5:9) applied to much more than idolatry. And Christianity echoed it with the famous text: "It is a fearful thing to fall into the hands of the living God" (Heb. 10:31). The same attitude appears in Homer, Hesiod, and the Greek tragedians. Universally men have had rituals to placate their personalizations of the *tremendum's* horror. Sacrifices, purifications, Ave Maria, *ora pro nobis,* all the schemes and days of atonement, give a relative security from divine wrath.

In the higher religions man has gone beyond this, as the Israelites early did. For in the same sentence in which God declared vengeance upon malefactors who hate him, he goes on to say, "but showing steadfast love to thousands of those who love me and keep my commandment." The whole is a projection of the old stern father who was kind to obedient children but vicious in punishing the disobedient ones. The only escape from the terror of his discipline was in his love, and the greatest discovery of the higher religions, psychologically as well as theologically, is that "Perfect love casteth out fear" (I John 4:18). "For God so loved the world that he gave his only begotten Son that whosoever believeth in him should not perish but have everlasting life" (John 3:16). The fear is still there, for by indirection, but still very directly, it is said that those who do not accept God's terms will "perish." God is still the damning God. We repress the basic religious terror only as we love God and accept his love. Religious love does not really cast out fear but only represses it. If we lose the sense of God's loving us, the old God of terror at once rises to horrify us. Winning God's love by accepting God's love and loving him in return becomes then, essentially the best form of placating God's wrath. The methods of placating God can be very different. If we believe that we can be safe from the *tremendum* only by offering it the pulsing hearts of human and animal beings, our way of life and sense of values will not at all resemble those of people who believe that God's in his heaven and all's right with the world and that we can forget all the divine punishments, or sanctions, as we sing *sanctus, sanctus, sanctus* in grateful response to a God of love. If man throughout history has generally been more anxious to keep out of God's hands than to feel safe in his arms, we must admit that love is for man at least the most constructive form of appeasement. In some rare religious geniuses, such as Socrates, the Buddha, and Gandhi, perfect love may indeed almost be said to have cast out fear. But I have never known such a man or woman personally and can say that when love is an incentive in religion at all it is usually as much the reverse of terror on the same coin as it is in the quotation I just made from Yahweh. My sainted mother used to tell me that we must indeed fear "sin."

It is useful also to see that religious experiences can arise through either the life or death instinct, as Freud called them. We have been talking from the point of view of the life instinct, the id, which wants to preserve itself from the extinction threatened by the tremendum, religions that look for a happy life here and hereafter. In many religious experiences, however, the death urge, thanatos, takes over. The craving to die in Christ that he may live in us is a different experience from the craving to wear a crown of glory in this life and in heaven. The two experiences may, of course, be deeply mixed in any one individual, but the religion of death, if I may call it so, can quite take over in its desire to vanish in God or the universal. We think of this primarily in association with Eastern mysticism, where one hopes eventually to be dissolved in Brahma or Nirvana. Terror of the *tremendum* becomes like vertigo, a solution of the horror of the emptiness beneath a great height by a craving to plunge down into it. The two types of experience appear in both East and West. I was one who got a vertiginous ecstasy singing

> Oh to be nothing, nothing,
> Only to lie at His feet,
> A broken and emptied vessel,
> For the Master's use made meet.

But though this does not go so far as reabsorption in Nirvana, even my Methodist fellows rarely sang this as their favorite hymn, if they sang it at all. On the other hand, the great mass of Hindus and Buddhists have not the slightest anticipation of being absorbed; religion becomes for them a matter of temple rituals so that one may accumulate enough merit to appear in the next incarnation in a somewhat better state. That is, they assert the id as do we Westerners. But the religion of personal glory as over against that of personal extinction illustrates in what utterly different ways the religious impulse has expressed itself. Actually, both are looking for security.

Legalism

The religious impulse, indeed, expresses itself in far more varieties than William James ever suggested. For example, he never alludes to the religion of legalism, an all-pervasive type that centers in obedience to definite statutes. For Moslems, Brahmans, orthodox Jews, and Calvinist Protestants man's piety is essentially measured by observance of the code, and every religion is full of it. The orthodox Jew says of his fellow, "He is a very pious man. He will not answer the phone on the Sabbath." My Protesant seniors used to say that I was a good boy because I did not drink, smoke, or swear. Obedience to Allah's commands is the very heart of Islam. Food tabus, in-marriage, and a thousand other requirements mark the proper Brahman. The point is that to do what we think is right is a great source of peace of mind, security, to most of the people in this room. "I could not live with myself if I did that" is something we would all consider very high motivation. And we all want to live at peace with ourselves. The superego, or conscience, or what you will, finds itself spelled out in the religious code, and we get peace of mind, or anxiety and guilt, as we do or do not obey it. Society gives us many codes: those of business, the club, patriotism, scientific procedure, logic, as well as those we would more ordinarily associate with religion. The fact is, of course, that the code you really obey is the code of your real religion. You are probably a polytheist and obey several, and get security from them all.

Orthodoxy

Another great form of religion is what I call orthodoxy, the security one gets from a scheme of reality. Most of us are here on Star Island because we have seen the old schemes dissolve – through the emergence of historical criticism, nuclear physics, and the newly dawning biological sciences, to name but a few of the modern revolutions – and have none to put in their places. There has been much talk about the loss of purpose and meaning for the individual which these brought about. If we now bravely say that we have lost only illusions in losing the old schemes of reality for man, we have no less a sense that we have lost a blessed sense of security, one that our forebears, and many of our contemporaries, found in a creed, a philosophy, an entelechy, which for them was the final truth. This drive to understand can be on the level of the simplest myth, as that a primeval turtle created the world or that the world is governed by a group of gods like the Olympians; or it can rise to the most abstract metaphysical or theological abstraction, which I call polysyllabic mythology. All bring the security of freedom from doubt. The great classic of this form of religion is Newman's *Apologia,* in which certainty of knowledge appears as his passionate goal from early years. When he found certainty in the Roman Catholic Church he for the first time came into real peace. At the end he almost purrs that since he entered the Church, "a thousand difficulties do not make a doubt." We have this sort of religious experience, or at least our radicals do, in political creeds also. We liberals, who still doubt many things, quite lack the sureness of touch of the Communists and the Birchers. It is the segregationists of the deep South, not we advocates of equal rights for all citizens, who quite confidently know where they should go and what is the next step. It is the attitude of commitment that here again makes an experience religious, not the value and actual truth of the belief to which we are committed. The peace that comes from such commitment is what the old people referred to when they talked on the consolations of religion.

Beauty

Many people also find their deepest religious experience in aesthetic gratifications. Presented with works of beauty they find themselves exalted, and with a sense of value and meaning. Religions of almost all sorts utilize this type of experience as they use music, pageantry, color, and architectural design. To our emotions (and this is what we are talking about all along) beauty becomes truth and the good, and often leads us to experience them in a way that words, theories, and laws do not. When I was a young man at Oxford I used to attend the services in the cathedral with breathless delight. I was almost at the point of joining up with them when one Sunday I heard the seraphic murmur of the boys' choir chanting Psalm 137: "O daughters of Babylon ... Happy shall he be that taketh and dasheth thy little ones against the rocks." A world of beauty suddenly vanished from me. I mentioned it that afternoon at tea to a theological don. He commented, "Oh, you listen to the words!" He went for the beauty, as do many who love the symbolism and ritual of the great churches and to whom the words have little importance. In its spell they have their religious experience. Beauty in poetry, ritual, and the plastic arts are themselves the source, the being, of religious experience for many, and will always be so. For as they immerse themselves in a beautiful form they feel their own formlessness, which is terror, take on beautiful form, which is peace.

Religious experience can also come to us through devotion to fellowmen and social justice. Others find it in patriotism, loyalty to their inner group; still others in the family, in the love of one's mate, in devotion to one's heart's desire, whatever that may be. Some devotion is a purely selfish delight in one's own good fortune, like James's healthy-minded people. Mysticism, in which James found the highest religious experience, I have already mentioned as the *Religionswissenschaft* that in its final form seeks self-dissolution by identifying one's existence with the great *tremendum* itself. Patterns of redemption and purification dominate other experiences when the *tremendum* invades one and sinks one in guilt. To these James's conversion experiences belong.

These patterns are ever with us. The varieties of religious experience are varied indeed. Men have killed their firstborn in order to placate the *tremendum,* have beaten themselves with lashes, starved themselves from food and sex, in the tragic conviction that they would be safer from the malevolence of the universe and of other men if they anticipated their torture by torturing themselves. Or they have set up phalli or phallic figures or had sacred intercourse in temples in order to share in divine love.

Beneath the Varieties

In all these the common denominator is devotion, commitment, service to the tremendum, the attempt in one way or another to placate it, appease it, even to declare that it is a source of beauty and love, anything so that men could have peace of mind, walk through the valley of the shadow of death and fear no evil. For this men have fought their bitterest wars, done the most ghastly crimes, as well as have risen to the greatest heights of sacrificial devotion. It is the devotion that makes a religion, not the face that the devotion pledges itself to this rather than that or expresses itself thus rather than so.

Hunger, thirst, cold, sex – and *Religionswissenschaft* – these are the universals. Insofar as we have any sense of direction or value in life we are all, for better or worse, religious.

Reformation of Religious Blueprints

The meaning of the Institute on Religion in an Age of Science lies not in our concern about better science but in our sense that science has destroyed the old mythological structure of the religions of the West and that we do not know how we as individuals or a civilization are to go on from here. I should like to close by pointing out still another great division in types of religious experience. I call these two the blueprint type and the creative type. The vast majority of men have lived, and presumably will always live, by blueprints. Tradition in the tribe or church, we have indicated, has transmitted the proper codes for legalism and ritual, the proper myths or theologies, the objects and forms of symbols and art, in terms of which men could understand their place in the universe and give their lives meaning. If many have found more security in their bank books than in their prayer books, both have required an acceptance of standards and a pattern of faith. The modern mind has discovered that not only the gods and myths of others but the theological traditions of our own are the products of human wishes, fears, and dreams.

In such a case we see we must turn, not to the traditions that have grown up about the great religious geniuses of the past, or to their own time-conditioned teachings, but to the men themselves as men. We see that the great ones did not live in blueprints at all but by their own creativity. The religion of aestheticism, for example, can take the form of one's being moved by the painting, architecture, poetry, or music of others, which is the blueprint approach, or by painting, designing, and writing poetry or music oneself. Wallace Stevens, the brilliant poet, was sent poems by writers from all over the world. He said he never read them, since the danger of unconscious imitation was too great. If others wanted to read his poems, very well; but it is clear that the one thing he treasured was writing for and out of himself. Every great genius, including every great religious genius, has essentially done the same. Like Amos they have thundered their own ethical idealism in terms of "Thus saith the Lord"; or like Jesus they have countered "But *I* say unto you." The followers of such a creative genius have turned him into a blueprint, but Gandhi and Francis of Assisi created their own values.

We are living now in one of the greatest, if not the greatest, creative ages in history. Men are so rapidly tossing out the old in science to create new working hypotheses that a man who leaves his work for as much as ten years to be a dean can almost never catch up and create in science again. At the same time, less rapidly than in science but still in such speed as the world has never seen, a worldwide social revolution is going on. The myth of white supremacy will long be repeated in some places but is as much exploded as the seven-days creation in Genesis. The myth is also passing that we must still call a marriage holy wedlock even though, after all possible attempts to make it so have failed, it actually remains "holy deadlock." The great blueprints of man are blanching out in our hands. Our ultra-conservatives still see the genius of American civilization in "free enterprise," that is, the right of the individual to make and keep as much money and power for himself as he can get, in any way he can get it, a conception that logically leads to anarchy. At the other extreme stand those who think that the purpose of our government should be the greatest good for the greatest number, an idea that logically comes out in socialism or communism. The man in the middle who wants neither of these must himself create his ideals and live without a formula.

We must live creatively, think creatively about man's inner and outer life, not sit wringing our hands, lamenting that natural science is advancing so much faster than spiritual understanding. If we do not create new spiritual and ethical values, we have no one to blame but ourselves.

And how do we go about doing so? By giving our real devotion to what we think is truly constructive for ourselves and society. In this way alone can we carry on the best in religion, and so can we be deeply religious in our science. For on this level all science becomes religious, that is, in its devotion to and application of the best it can discover. The great ones will be creative in their devotion; but they will never forget the principle by which science has introduced a new epoch in human evolution, that personal conviction must always be subject to correction in terms of new data or knowledge.

Star Island will never produce any single formula or model for reconciling religion with the new contents of physics, genetics, psychology, or social structure. We do not write blueprints here. In the new world our task at present is to make new forms for ourselves as we find the old ones, by which the mass of men will continue to live, do not meet our personal needs. If we ourselves no longer believe that the God of Einstein's universe is counting the hairs of our heads, or stands ready to move mountains into the sea if we ask it with sufficiently commanding a faith, the simple fact remains that we can still pray, can break down the pettiness of our ordinary lives in the reality of what seems to us a transcendent good. Socrates was killed, among other reasons, for taking the gods of Athens too lightly, but he never lost the vivid experience of the little presence within him. I do not speak of religion in terms of an organization designed to propagate faith in a tradition but in terms of the still small voice in our hearts. Many great scientists obviously live by this, while they cut, destroy, and build anew.

Security? We may find it as we create fresh patterns of thought, conduct, value, emotional responses. But we must never seek the full security of an opiate, as Marx called traditional blueprints. But the great creative dreams of Marx became themselves an opiate as his followers turned them into programs and dogmas. All creative dreams become opiates when they seem so true that they stupefy our individual creative criticism, however much they may inspire to action, as does Marxism, or lull people's minds in peace. I can read no other lesson from the religious experiences of mankind, at least for us, but that out of the ruins of the old, together with the new knowledge, we must have the courage to create again. If in the spirit of modern thinking we know we can now create only working hypotheses, formulations of perhaps temporary pragmatic value, then let us create working hypotheses of hope and meaning and create ourselves anew in the process. We live both as scientists and human beings, not by the permanent value of our creations, but by the very act of creating. How our creations will be represented in later blueprints does not concern us. In the new age we must pray, even though we no longer know to what or whom we pray, pray that in all humility we have the courage to live devoted to what seems best for us and for all men. Religion at its highest has given men security as they have sought the best they could find and ascribed that best to the *tremendum*. If our ancestors did this as dogma, we must do the same as working hypothesis, but with no less devotion.

The best scientists I know assure me that the laws of science are all human formulations subject to correction, formulas that we project upon the world and find that they take us a long way in controlling it. Certainly the patterns of cause and effect in human history, by which we understand and use the past, are, I assure you, human projections. So we must admit that our values, goals, and standards are not divine revelations but are our own imperfect creations, while we still believe in them and live by them as Wallace Stevens believed in his poetry and as we trust the working hypotheses of science when we fly in a plane. Else we are little children who, having built castles with our blocks, have dashed them down in glorious destruction, then stood and wept for what we have lost. Our old castles are gone, but the blocks remain, the blocks of human creativity. We have come to Star Island each to put a few of his own blocks together.

Chapter Three

The Bible as Product of the Ancient World

*Five Essays on the Bible. Papers Read at the 1960 Meeting
of the American Council of Learned Societies*
(New York, 1960: American Council of Learned Societies), 1-19

From the world of the ancient Near East and the Mediterranean only one Bible has survived, that is, a collection of inspired writings which together form the basis of a religion. We still have Homer and Hesiod, indeed, but however much the Greeks generally revered and quoted them, along with the other poets and dramatists, they never collected or canonized their writings as forming together a unique revelation of God. We know that other ancient religions had their *hieroi logoi,* as they were called in hellenistic and Roman times, books or texts which contained the sacred myths, songs, passwords, and rituals of a group; and a few, like the sacred texts of Egypt, have been preserved. But our Bible alone has kept its authority. It has done so because its inherent character produced religious movements and organizations which two thousand years, the most changing millennia in human history, could not destroy. On the contrary, deeply as Greece and Rome have affected modern civilization, they do not present us with anything analogous to the social reality of Judaism or Christianity because the Classicists, often as they have indulged themselves in dreams of a long-lost perfection, have no Bible. Christian Science and Mormonism could do what classical studies could not, as they too put a bound book of the truth into pious hands. Christianity would hardly have come into existence as a formal movement at all if the early Christians had not so passionately clung to the Bible of the Jews (in Greek translation, of course) and justified their doing so by asserting that all the basic points of their own teaching only fulfilled ancient biblical prophecy and intent. Jesus' criticism of the law of the Jews had to begin with the assurance that he was not destroying it but fulfilling it, and by cursing anyone who would alter so much as the dot on an *I,* or the cross on a *T,* to paraphrase his own reference to the Hebrew alphabet. Early Christians claimed to be the true Israel and, by reading Christian soteriology into the Jewish Bible, had a basis on which they could build their own religious structure. Jews felt very much about the Christian biblical interpretations as orthodox Christians now do about the New Testament interpretations of Mrs. Eddy; that is, they felt that the new movement was spoiling all that was essential in the true ancient biblical teaching, but their feeling made the Christian claim no less confident or effective. So even today, one of the most important functions of the Bible is to keep the ancient world vivid in people's minds, to keep subsequent ages aware of their ancient roots.

My task, however, is not to discuss the general phenomenon of biblicalism or traditionalism in history, but to consider how the Bible has preserved aspects of the civilizations of the past. No one will expect that a single paper will appraise a body of literature in which, with the single exception of the first century B.C., experts find original compositions of every century from the thirteenth or twelfth century B.C. to the first or second century A.D. The sources of ideas in the biblical writings add to these many more centuries indeed and take us from Egypt, Mesopotamia, and Persia to Greece and Alexandria. When archeologists discovered the ancient Ugaritic poems of the Canaanites, poems that go back to the third millennium, they found much of what the writers of the Old Testament throughout the first millennium denounced in content, but copies in form. In the Old Testament we have the supreme products of ancient Near Eastern poetry, historiography, and, above all, religious idealism.

The Old Testament, however, only indirectly tells us about the life and times of ancient Palestine; it directly records the developing ideals of a small part of the ancient Hebrews and Israelites. This group could finally bring it about that such men as Elijah and Amos became national heroes, but in their own day these prophets had said, "I, even I only, am left." As Abraham departed from Ur of the Chaldees, and Moses brought the people out of Egypt, the story of the Hebrews is that of a few men of spiritual genius who tried to lead a rebellious people away from the conceptions of their neighbors. The other civilizations of the ancient world, to all appearances, suffered no such divided loyalties. In general, throughout the East the priests and teachers really represented the people and their aspirations before the gods. Not so with the Israelites. According to the story, Moses dragged a constantly complaining people through the desert, a people who, even while he was having his ecstasy with God on Sinai set up the golden calf. The great king Solomon openly cultivated the gods of his neighbors, as did most of his successors in both Israel and Judah. Against this the prophets fulminated, and some of the priests. But the masses of the Jews (like most people today) were ready to accept any myths and worship that would console them and give them peace of mind. The great cycle of Jewish festivals and the old temple rituals and sacrifices are for the most part palpable adaptations of pagan usages. The process continued into the hellenistic period, when in accepting Greco-Syrian forms and divine names for worship the Jews of high and low society went in my opinion much beyond even what Josephus and the books of Maccabees tell us. The idea that the Jews as a group throughout their early history detested the religious practices of their neighbors exaggerates and distorts the true fact: the Jews, for the most part, were ready to worship in their neighbors' fashions; yet amazingly they produced the great idealists, whose dreams the people came finally to recognize and accept, so that the writings of these religious geniuses, their very denunciations of the lives of the general run of ancient Hebrews, became the guide and inspiration of later generations of Jews and Christians alike.

To demonstrate in what way the Old Testament both represents and rejects the civilization of the ancient Near East is quite beyond the scope of this paper. We may stop to consider only two aspects of the subject, attitudes toward God and toward law. The Old Testament obviously develops many other themes, but we may safely say that God and his law dominate them all.

The Old Testament God

As to the idea of God, Judaism was to give to later civilizations a monotheism formed by exclusion rather than inclusion. It is familiar that for the God of Abraham, Isaac, and Jacob, who finally got the single proper name of Yahweh, the Hebrews originally claimed only that he was the special god of their group. All the civilizations of antiquity began with a pantheon of their own gods, usually with a supreme god, such as Ashur or Zeus, as their rulers. From this two separate paths were taken to monotheism. At first, by one path, a figure like Zeus would emerge as the really dominating force among the gods of the tribal or national pantheon, superior, for example, to Hera and Athena. Ashur seems to have won out for the Assyrians and Marduk for the Babylonians. This process really produced a monotheism when people reduced all their gods to being aspects and forms of revelation of the one God. Herin the Stoic Hymn to Zeus and the Orphic Hymns resembled the tablet of Marduk, where "Enlil is Marduk with reference to ruling and decision, Sin is Marduk as illuminator of the night, Shamash is Marduk as God of Justice,"[1] and the like. Later much the same was said in another tablet to make all the gods manifestations of another claimant to divine supremacy, Ninurta. Even as far back as the Pyramid texts the process was going on in Egypt. The texts say almost nothing of Osiris that in some way or another they do not say of Ra or Atum. Always gods are mentioned by special names, but only modern scholars ever tried to define consistent differences in function to correspond to those names. Which name a given worshiper or temple would choose to give supreme honors seems to have been a fortuitous choice. The names and personalities of the lesser gods were kept, but their existence tended to become like that of the persons of the Trinity in the later Christian heresies of modalistic monotheism.

Such monotheism could be developed as a national or tribal affair, but usually it had also to include foreign deities. What we ordinarily call syncretism means the recognition of the gods of other people along with one's own gods, a process usually accomplished by saying such things as that Venus, Aphrodite, Ishtar, Astarte, and Isis are different, local names for a single deity. By

---

[1]W.F. Albright, *From the Stone Age to Christianity* (2d ed.; 1957), p. 217.

combining the two processes a cosmic monotheism could develop, though it was more apt to turn into a sort of pantheism, in which the identify of divine persons perished in an all-absorbing Ultimate that tended to lose personality altogether. The great empires of the past, Babylonian, Persian, Greek, and Roman, could achieve peace and some measure of unity in civilization only as they could thus recognize the value of their own and other people's local myths and divine figures and transcend them all. In terms of modern myths and ultimates, the problem of world peace is the same today.

Throughout its history the Jewish leaders resisted such an approach to peace. Jesus was never more truly a Jew than when he said, "I came not to bring peace, but a sword." For Jewish leaders and the Christian and Moslem leaders who descended from them gave to the world a monotheism of exclusion. Most Jews obviously tried the other paths, that of such frank syncretism as must have lain behind the inclusiveness of Solomon, or that which made Yahweh the commanding figure over the gods of other people, the "judge among gods" (Psalms 82:1) or "a great King above all gods" (Psalms 95:3). But the attitude which won out among Jews simply regards the gods of other nations as illusions of the gentiles, whose images have no divine reality within them or beyond them, and whose worship is a travesty of true piety. The great confession of the Jews, "Hear, O Israel: Yahweh is our God, Yahweh alone," achieved on this path by exclusion, insisting that my god is the only God: If you do not worship what and as I do, you are an idolater, a heathen, words which have meaning only to those whose approach to monotheism is by exclusion.

Many people have discussed the values of Jewish monotheism, but only those praise it who personally follow it in its Jewish, Christian, or Moslem forms. A monotheism developed by exclusion has its logical and inevitable concommitant in a desire to destroy the false conception of others, whether by missions or by the swords of all religious wars, just as it created the only rebellious political center in the great Pax Romana of the first and second centuries after Christ. The God of the Old Testament had become in their sight the one God, creator and ruler of the universe and all that is within it, while he remained the personal Yahweh of the Jews. Here indeed the Bible records one of the most extraordinary and powerful creations of the ancient world. If I must add that exclusiveness in religion seems to me at times one of the greatest sources of evil known to man, the sense of one's own rightness as over against the horrible error of others, still we must admit the amazing potency of the Jewish attitude in modern civilization.

The Old Testament Law

The Jewish Bible also presents us with a unique contribution in preserving ancient law. Hebrew laws can often be paralleled in the laws of other ancient peoples. Problems of torts; of the security of property from theft, malice, or careless damage; of deposit; of slavery; of keeping one's wife or wives safe from other men; of marriage and eligibility for marriage; of divorce; of the sanctity of oaths (primitive contract) – all these appear in much the same forms in various codes of the time. The Jewish code resembles in many points that of the early Mesopotamians, but no more than both do the Greek. Actually when the Jews came out into the Roman world they had relatively little difficulty in interpreting their old laws in terms of Greek and Roman jurisprudence, a process we can see vividly in Philo, and one which is being increasingly recognized as actively influencing the later development of rabbinic law.

Ancient states had always had religious sanction. A king was by definition a divine person, or one especially sacred to God; his function was, as in ancient China, to represent the people before God. He was also supposed, in a unique way, to know the will of God or the gods, or that vague "right" which might be called, among many things, the law of nature. Even when the state seemed secular and the officials were chosen by ballot, as in Athens, the business of the state was quite as importantly to conduct the proper worship of the gods as to keep the peace among its citizens. And the law of even these states was sacred. Minos in Crete, Lycurgos in Sparta, and to a lesser extent Solon in Athens, were quasi-divine figures in the popular mind, who gave the citizens not laws of their own contriving, but formulations of the divine law. Roman lawyers of the Empire increasingly used religion to sanction the emperor and the law itself.

In the persistence of this sort of thinking, the continued influence of the Old Testament has played a large role, for there was an authoritative, revealed statement of the law of God. The Bible as finally canonized told men with indisputable authority that Moses got from God the laws of cultus, sacrifice, priesthood, food, inheritance, marriage, torts, criminal law, and judicial procedure all in one package, along with ethics and exhortations to moral idealism. The Hebrew "Torah" was correctly translated "law" so long as law was supposed to cover all these matters and be the teaching of God to men.

The modern world has increasingly tried to separate Church and State, the sacred and profane, by asserting that traditional revelation has no bearing upon or relation to the conduct of law and government. Those of you who know the history of this problem best will know how deeply the working out of a secular State has always been challenged by the biblical tradition living on in the Churches and hearts of most men of the West. Marxists have tried to clear the air by discarding the bible and all traditional forms of religious organization and cult. Whether they will eventually succeed, or will have to make concessions to the bible, with its Christian and Jewish conception of divine rule, or have not really continued it under new terminology, I shall not say. All I am pointing out is that the old Testament still keeps alive in modern society one of the most important aspects of antiquity, the conception that law and government never cease to be divine prerogatives, even when administered in executive mansions and human courts; that the distinction between the sacred and profane, made by many scholars the very definition of religion, is an artificial distinction, a recent and modern one. As long as the Old Testament carries on its influence, the ancient unity of divine and human rulership and law will continue to assert itself. Both sides, the ancient and modern, have much compelling to say. As one who is by no means an ecclesiastic I fear very deeply the power for evil of individuals or institutions which try to conduct the affairs of men in terms of a special knowledge that they have of divine will or cosmic right. Yet courts of law which support precedent *qua* precedent and ignore dreams of men for justice and mercy can be quite as destructive. If Old Testament law seems to us often antiquated and useless, it has recorded for us as no other document has the ancient dream of a society and a law which would not call ultimate the fallible judgments of human beings. We moderns who believe inhuman judgment must also believe in a better society than any we have ever seen and work for it, else our very institutions will shrivel of dry rot. For this we shall find inspiration in Aristotle, the Roman legists, the Greek democracies (at their best), but also in Sinai, and in the prophets' impassioned dreams of justice and mercy as recorded in the Old Testament.

The New Testament

The New Testament is an utterly different book. It must have been composed within a century at the most, and more probably in half that time. Like all human productions, its ultimate roots include all the ages not only of the Old Testament proper, but of untold millennia of human development. But it records how the teachings of an extraordinary person, Jesus of Nazareth, affected a little group of people, and how their lives were transformed by his death and by their confident belief that they had seen him risen from the dead. These writings became a Bible in themselves, because the later Church believed that this group of people had had a contact with God, a divine revelation, of a sort which has never been repeated. Church tradition early explained the diverse points of view of these writings by the different problems to which they were addressed, but it has always regarded them all equally as the ultimate composition of the Holy Spirit and expressions of the mind and purpose of the one God.

For the last century and a quarter historical criticism has said other things. To historical critics the differences have seemed basically those of the personalities of the authors, or of local traditions, and hence the books have seemed the product not of a single divine Spirit but of a diversity of human spirits. Historical critics have by no means begun, or come through, with a single theory of the relation of these books to one another, or of the character of the early Church or churches which produced them. I shall not catalogue and review the various schools and points of view of New Testament critics, but rather I shall describe for the first time the point of view I have myself reached, and which I propose, after the details of the work I am now doing are disposed of, to spend my remaining years in elucidating. If my approach is ever accepted at all, it will never seem adequate to anyone, including myself. Those of you who know the various approaches to New Testament study will anticipate that what I shall say will by no means be entirely novel. But much as I have learned from former scholars, or should have learned, as a whole I have never encountered what was for me a satisfactory approach to the problem of the origin of the New Testament and with it of the origin of the Christian Church.

The difficulty seems to me to lie in the simplicity necessary, apparently, for the scholarly mind. The scientist with his controlled experiments, with his exclusion of uncontrolled variables, shows by his results what great value lies in simplicity. As our data become more diversified, difficulties of explanation increase in geometrical proportion. We can understand only as we specialize, as we develop a simple approach to more limited material. Historians prefer to simplify their data by putting them into chronological and hence causal relations. This leads to that. It is hard to see how better man can give form to the disorder of the past as we learn of it in scattered documents.

The method in general has produced such extraordinary results that I am deeply committed to it, but it has its dangers when carried too far. In the history of ideas, especially where we have only occasional documents, as we do for the ancient world, the tendency is to date ideas by the document in which we first find them, and then to suppose that later documents which express similar ideas must directly or indirectly have been influenced by the earlier document and its writer. Or we may suppose that a document which we can date must precede and influence another document which we cannot otherwise date but which has similar ideas. So if we can find some ideas in Luke or Mark which resemble some ideas expressed by Paul, we conclude that Luke or Mark must have read Paul or been influenced by his teaching, because we know Paul was early, while the date of the gospels is highly disputed. Philological historians tend to be particularly susceptible to this fallacy. It is much more comfortable to move from document to document, one often feels, than to presuppose common sources which have been lost. Still more nebulous does it seem to postulate an atmosphere behind documents, in which ideas were being talked about freely and different individuals were presenting them similarly but by no means identically. Actually, in two documents the more complex statement of ideas may be much earlier than the more simple, or the reverse may be true. A well-coordinated statement of an idea may indeed be contemporary with a popular misstatement of it, each quite independent of the other as documents.

Closely related to this is the historical fallacy, rarely stated explicitly, that an earlier document about either ideas or a historical incident will more correctly report the true events or original teachings than a later document. The fallacy appeared in New Testament criticism a century ago, when critics who doubted the validity of the tradition of Jesus' teaching tended to date the Gospels late, while the orthodox, without such doubts, usually dated them early. Actually the date of the composition of a Gospel has nothing direct to tell us at all about the validity of its material. The assumption of coordination between early date and reliability of information usually operates, if unconsciously, even today.

Another fallacy is to assume that people in a given ancient city thought alike, so that the hellenistic aspects of the Fourth Gospel presuppose that the Gospel was written in Ephesus, as the Church Fathers suggested, especially because some seven centuries before the Gospel could have been written Heraclitus had used the word Logos in Ephesus (though with a meaning utterly different from that of the Fourth Gospel). In contrast, the thinking in Jerusalem must have been overwhelmingly "Jewish," it is supposed, and since we know of no document definitely written in Jerusalem which discussed the Logos or other ideas from Greek philosophers, such subjects could have had no influence or place there. Little consideration has been given to the know fact that Acts reports hellenistic synagogues as being in Jerusalem itself and as playing an important part in Christian beginnings. In them men might have been using the word Logos quite as freely, perhaps far more so, than the Jews in Ephesus. Jews in Jerusalem thought quite differently from those in Alexandria, this fallacy assumes, and all Jews in each city thought alike, so that "Alexandrian" Judaism was quite different from "Palestinian" Judaism.

Further, we have not a good understanding of the danger of arguing *e silentio*. We all accuse our opponents of doing so, when as a matter of fact we all do it and must do it, if we try to come to conclusions about matters for which we have no direct evidence. Pots need not cast aspersions at kettles in this matter. Any coherent account of the beginnings of Christianity must largely be a matter of bridges we ourselves build over the chasms of silence that surround and separate our documents. What we can and should do in circumstances is present our reconstructions as hypothetical suggestions rather than as assured facts, for we can all discuss hypothetical suggestions with a dispassion which we cannot use with unfounded ascertains of fact. We can discuss other people's hypothetical suggestions with dispassion, however, only if we are aware that our own ideas are also hypothetical and must be so, since to draw any conclusions at all in this field we must all argue largely from silence.

Finally there is the danger that in our ignorance of the past we project our own desires and patterns into the material when we try to interpret it. This, may I say, is worse than a danger – we do it more or less inevitably. I can talk as I just have done and shall do, about inconsistency in early Church thinking, collectively and individually, because I feel within myself no inner urge to consistency. A person with a more philosophic mind cannot stop with my tolerance of my own and other people's taking now one point of view, now another. Accordingly, what seems to me at least a partial understanding of the New Testament documents seems to a systematic thinker an admission of total failure, because understanding to him demands consistency. Nothing can heal this breach. The New Testament seems to me to have been written by people inconsistent with one another and with themselves; but it must seem basically consistent throughout to the systematic biblical theologian. Of course, I think in this that I am right, but insofar as I think so, I must admit that I am projecting my own *Denkweise* into the material, as, I am equally sure, the systematizers are doing.

The idea that Jesus, Paul, and John, individually or collectively, presented us with a consistent way of thinking is the modern survival of the fallacy of scholasticism. For the medieval scholastics, developing the faith of the fourth- and fifth-century theologians, supposed that since the Spirit must have spoken through the biblical writers and the early fathers and the creeds, it was possible to fit all into a single system. If modern non-Catholic scholars regard the supreme achievement of this movement, the *Summa* of Thomas, as only the greatest tour de force of the human mind, this has not prevented many of them from feeling that New Testament theology was a meaningful term in the singular, or that we shall find the real Paul, or the real John, in an abstract and homogeneous system. Actually not Plato, Aristotle, Philo, Plotinus, or any other ancient thinker ever dreamed of creating a system of philosophy or theology or of using terms with technically consistent meaning. This by no means prevents people interested in systems from trying to find consistency in the New Testament. As I said, my own disinterest in abstract consistency must be blinding me on my side. Projection cannot be avoided. Plotinus saw a great mystic in Plato, while the nineteenth century saw in him a great logical thinker. The ecclesiastic will be impressed by the scattered allusions in the New Testament to organization, sacraments, and disciplines, a Methodist or Congregationalist or agnostic will not. Like Luther, God help us, we can never be anything, ultimately, but ourselves.

With these dangers in mind, we may ask what the New Testament gives us and assume at the outset that it reports some of the life and extraordinary teachings of a man of simple background from Galilee in Palestine. It tells how this man was crucified, how at first a little group of his followers all saw him risen from the dead, and how this group grew to five hundred or more. New Testament history and the Christian movement may be taken to begin with this group conviction that the risen Jesus had been seen. Hence, it must be presumed that by his extraordinary personal character and teaching he made so profound an impression upon his simple followers that they thought that in their resurrection vision of him they had seen his real fleshly person, not simply a ghost. The vision transformed them from the cowardly people they seem to have been during Jesus' crucifixion into men fearless under torture and cruel execution. They formed themselves into a group and devoted themselves to telling their remarkable story to others and to spreading the contagion of their conviction that in Jesus man had found the solution of all problems. As he was raised from the dead so would his followers be. "For if the dead rise not, then Christ has not been raised; and if Christ be not raised your faith is vain; ye are yet in your sins" (I Corinthians 15:16 f.). His exact significance and character men were to debate for centuries, but all agreed that his person, and above all his resurrection, marked him as at least a special messenger from God who transcended all the revelations of God and of God's will in the past.

That the new Testament assures us that the early apostles were confident they had seen their remarkable teacher risen from the dead I do not see that we can doubt. Only those can demur who regard the whole collection of writings as a pious fraud, deny the existence of Jesus altogether, and think his character a pure creature of some genius who wanted to make vivid and put into the world of historical record a dying and rising savior of the type popular in pagan religions of the time. But the New Testament presents so extraordinarily diverse a group of documents and interpretations of his significance that the master mind which originated the fraud does not appear at any point, did not conceivably exist.

A beautiful story about Jesus tells how when he made his triumphant entry into Jerusalem the people of the city asked, "Who is this?" The multitude who had accompanied him answered simply, "This is Jesus, the prophet of Nazareth of Galilee" (Matthew 21:10f.). After the resurrection appearances, however, that answer was too simple, Jesus must have been more than this, his followers felt, and apparently the earliest account of his superhuman character puts its beginning at the baptism, for then Jesus saw the heavens opened and heard a voice which, it seems likely according to the original account, said, "Thou art my beloved son: This day have I begotten thee" (Mark 1:11).[2] This tradition, basically that of Mark, then went on to show how Jesus manifested his superhuman character largely through miracles and how he foretold his return as the heavenly avenger who would cause heaven and earth to pass away, but who would set up a new order in which the righteous would take part. Here we have a resolution that requires the destruction of the present cosmos, an idea quite foreign alike to older Jewish tradition, in which God found his creation good, and to Greek tradition, in which the world was essentially indestructible and eternal (except for the Stoic cosmic cycles, to which this formulation bears no resemblance). It was, however, fully at home in the Iranian world where the great problem of Ohrmuzd with his creation, as Ahriman had corrupted it, could be solved only by its destruction and a fresh beginning. We know from eschatological books that this Iranian point of view had become mingled in Jewish hopes with the typical Jewish Messiah, who would have been only a political and imperial conqueror. But nothing we have outside the New Testament shows as clearly how passionately the dream of the cosmic Messiah had taken popular hold when thus fused with the Jewish political hope. Mark also delighted in reporting brief sayings of Jesus and the way in which he assumed legal authority beyond that of the Pharisees. All these are clearly part of a Jewish point of view.

---

[2]The Voice from heaven says this in the gospel of the Ebionites, as quoted by Epiphanius. See M.R. James, *The Apocryphal New Testament* (1924), p. 9. Since this only completes the quotation from Psalms 2:7, I have always thought it the original form of the tradition.

"Jesus the son of God," given in its simplest form in Mark, was a phrase to produce one of the most momentous disputes of history as it came to demand explanation from later metaphysical Christians. In early years, however, it quickly got a mythical, or storied, explanation, perhaps one introduced to match and outdo the story of how God intervened to produce the birth of Jesus' slightly older contemporary, John the Baptist. John's birth was described after the manner of such old Jewish traditions as that of the birth of Isaac and Samuel, in which God at last opens the womb of a barren woman so that she can conceive. Luke tells this story of John, but only to go one better for Jesus' birth, to claim that in producing the superhuman man God not only miraculously opened a female womb so that it could become pregnant, but himself fertilized it. This pattern had a hoary history in the begetting of kings of Egypt and the great heroes in Greek tradition; both Plato and Alexander the Great, to name only two, were traditionally thus conceived. By what channels it came to be told of Jesus we do not know. No historian is in a position to say that Jesus was not thus conceived, any more than he is in a position to say that Plato and Alexander were not begotten by gods; but from the point of view of historical evidence, he can say that no one of the three accounts is better established than the others. We must argue from silence if, noticing that neither Mark, Paul, nor John mentions the Virgin Birth, we conclude that they had not heard of it. Inasmuch, however, as each in his own way was eager to demonstrate Jesus' superhuman character, the presumption must be that they would at least have alluded to it had they known it. For once the story was accepted, it became rapidly, if not at once, one of the cornerstones of Christian teaching.

If the Virgin Birth was not the earliest way of accounting for the special character of the risen Lord, the story, unless it was an actual event, must have come from people who had been accustomed to think in this way and who belonged to first-generation, or early second-generation, Christianity. No one, we may also safely presume, ever put his finger to his forehead and decided that if the pagan tradition of divine begetting were asserted for Jesus, it would make the strongest possible statement of his divine character and then went on deliberately to attach the story to him. As told both in Matthew and Luke, the account of the birth of Jesus does not read like either an Egyptian or Greek story of the begetting of a savior by a divinity. It is Greek or Egyptian in idea, but thoroughly Hebraized in form and atmosphere, and would seem to have come from some Jews who had long been thinking of their Jewish heroes in these terms. We know of such Jews from Philo, who had magnified the Patriarchs and Moses into superhuman Saviors of man and had told of the special divine begetting of Isaac and Moses to explain their characters. The New Testament seems to record in the Virgin Birth, accordingly, a lost but important aspect of classical antiquity, as it was spreading out even into Judaism. Because the story, with its emotional impact, survives to the present, it presumably has kept alive the emotional and religious value of the conception in pagan antiquity as the pagan myths have not themselves done.

The first or second generation of Christians also produced other explanations of the superhuman character of Jesus. Paul, as I have said, seems to have operated without benefit of this tradition. To him Jesus was made from the seed of David according to the flesh and declared to be the Son of God, with power, according to the spirit of holiness, by the resurrection of the dead (Romans 1:3 f.). But if Paul does not mention Jesus' mother, we know that at the end he considered Jesus to be one who had existed in the form of God, indeed equal to God, but one who took on the likeness of men in humility and then was again exalted by God above every name (Philippians 2:6-10; cf., Collossians 3:9-15). In these phrases, Paul shows similarly a conception of a "Form of God" which existed apart from God and which could become incarnate as a human being, or, as he says elsewhere, "born of a woman" (Galatians 4:4). Paul is not reflecting the story of the Virgin Birth but paralleling it by applying to Jesus the more metaphysical and less mythical conception of how God intervenes to save men – a conception basically Greek or Hellenistic, and even more typically Philonic than the mythical statements. For to him Jesus brought a fresh infusion or form into a world become formless through sin.

The Virgin Birth stories introduce documents which go onto describe Jesus much in Markan terms, though they give a far richer collection both of the beautiful parabolic teachings and of his claims to superior legal authority. But none of the synoptics makes what Paul and John and Hebrews do of the idea that man is to share in the divine nature of Christ or be exalted with Christ beyond the limits of human nature. It is enough for the Synoptists that the saints will have a place in the world to come and in the resurrection to eternal life. Paul's point, on the contrary, is the identification of the believer with Christ – "Not I live, but Christ liveth in me" – the idea which, along with Paul's repudiation of the Torah as statutes, made the Jews repudiate the Christian movement. The hellenistic world assumed that man could be transformed and that, in putting on the garment of Isis or Osiris, he took on the divine nature of the god. The pagan world was at that time full of stories and rituals of apotheosis, of enthusiasm in its true sense, a state which could be achieved also through philosophy or mystical contemplation.

Apotheosis was no part of traditional Jewish teaching, and insofar as it required the mediation of God in a human body was anathema to Jews. But not to all Jews, we know from Philo, who himself hoped for mystical victory over his sinful nature and ultimate restoration to deity. So for Christians, Christ became not only the wonder person who would destroy this world and set up another, but also the divine power who would destroy sin within the individual and make him into a "saint." The records have Jesus say that the catastrophic end of the old order would occur "before this generation had passed" (Mark 13:30), and this doctrine Paul accepted. He also thought of Jesus as being the savior of individuals, and in Paul's brief career (if he was killed under Nero, he probably did not preach Christianity as an active missionary much more than ten years), the Savior of individuals displaced within his thinking almost entirely the heavenly and cosmic reformer. We have little reason to suppose that the same orientation must have taken place much later in the authors of the Fourth Gospel and of the Epistle to the Hebrews. As contrasted with the Hebrew *Denkweise* of the Synoptists, with their ethics and generally violent eschatology, stand these three writers with a view of Christianity not as a movement of society as a whole, but as a salvation by the transforming of individuals. They echo the primitive eschatological hope, but subordinate or lose it in a type of salvation that is basically Greek – basically, I may say, Platonic or late-Platonic. The writer to the Hebrews, who contrasted the reality of the things not seen with the unreality of the visible world, the struggle of Paul to keep the mind free of the dominance of the flesh, these did quite as much to keep Platonism a living force in future ages as any professional philosopher. Such changes would not necessarily have required a great deal of time. We know that Paul was early; I should guess the book of Revelation to be not much later than A.D. 70, if not earlier, perhaps the product of the stormy years of Gaius and Nero.

That is, I see no genetic development in the New Testament writings but a reflection of various responses within a single generation to the miracle of the resurrection vision. The responses presuppose a variety of background within Judaism itself. Jews must have been interested in such poetic and prophetic ethic as we have in the Sermon on the Mount and the parables; in such cool gnomic ethic as James made of Christianity; in a heavenly savior who would destroy this order, political and cosmic, to inaugurate at last the perfect creation of God; in a divine intervention in human form, which would show individual men the way, give them a new dynamic, so that they could be themselves changed into being the sons of God, made truly in his form or image.

Into other equally important aspects of the New Testament we cannot go. The little group very early developed a discipline of its members which centered in access to sacraments, without which a person could not be saved. For this also early Christians presumably would have had the example of an organization that had rites of its own, especially a rite of bread and wine, an organization, sharply disciplined, that expelled from the holy table those who did not conform to the standards of the administrator. We actually know that all these attitudes existed in Judaism, and from the Qumran sects by the Dead Sea we know that such organizations were active in Palestine itself. The different types of Christianity, which seem to have developed almost at once and to be reflected in the books of the New Testament, are best explained, not by a series of stages, with Christianity passing united from one stage to another, but as the almost simultaneous discovery by each type of Jew that the risen Lord fulfilled his own antecedent ideas and aspirations.

We must at once use the term "type of Jew" and beware of it. Each little group of eschatologists seems to have had its own formulation of hopes. Similarly, all hellenized Jews, apparently, by no means thought alike, any more than do all modern Reform Jews. Hellenized Jews could have been as divergent as Paul and John and still have been recognizably hellenized. Our terms, which we cannot do without, get terribly in our way. Every Catholic knows that there is no typical Catholic, every Jew that there is no typical Jew. The typical American or Englishman or even, I should suppose, with all their regimentation of education, the typical Russian are terms that we must abandon when we wish really to understand any of these people. In the same way, no New Testament author speaks as a typical hellenized Jewish-Christian or, to use G.F. Moore's fictional term, as a normative Jew. The individual is never the type. So, while we may see types of Judaism behind the Gospels and Epistles, we must also suppose that the documents were written by enraptured individuals in whom "types" were blended.

The Church preserved this burst of highly individual books with all their different points of view and made them into a single Bible. Here we have what we began with, the miracle of a canonical collection which, once accepted as such, was preserved with almost superhuman care for textual integrity. It put with this collection, as a single revelation of the one God, the books of the ancient Jews. Churchmen of all denominations have worked since that time on the endless problem of showing how they present a single faith. Faith that our problems are solved in the person of the risen Lord is the faith in which traditional Christianity unites, but the problems Jesus seemed to solve have essentially, from the very beginning, been each man's own. Jesus could become the model monk, crusader, public school gentleman, Marxist leader, captain, bridegroom through the ages, precisely because he was given so many roles from the start.

Obviously I have answered no question in this paper; most of the important questions about the New Testament are unanswerable. But I have at least stated my conviction that the Bible gathers together more aspects of antiquity than any one book I know, not even excepting the *Geography* of Strabo, and that they were preserved because the early Christians made these writings into a Bible.

Part Two

JUDAISM

Chapter Four

Literal Mystery in Hellenistic Judaism

Quantulacumque: Studies Presented to Kirsopp Lake by Pupils, Colleagues, and Friends, ed. R.P. Casey, S. Lake, and A.K. Lake (London, 1937), 227-241

In connection with my recent volume on the mystic gospel of Hellenistic Judaism there seems to have been much perplexity as to whether the terms "initiation," "mystery" and the like were being used "figuratively" or "literally." What has surprised me is that the question has been posed as a dilemma: was the Mystery of Hellenistic Judaism a real, a literal, mystery with rites, or was it only a figurative mystery without them? In reality, for centuries before Philo there had been talk among the Greeks of a literal mystery which had no rites at all, namely the mystery of philosophy.[1]

It is well known that the Pythagoreans were deeply influenced by Orphic ideas, and were organized on the model of mystic θίασοι, with hearers and an inner group of μαθηματικοί who were the only ones to whom the saving truths of the sect were revealed. The difficulty is that we cannot generalize about the way this inner teaching was regarded. It is a fair assumption, however, that the members of the inner group thought that their studies were leading to a genuine κάθαρσις of soul which would enable them to escape the cycle of recurrent incarnations.[2]

Heraclitus seems to have avoided mystic language no more than his followers. An ancient epigram quoted by Diogenes Laertius[3] said: "Be not in a hurry to finish the book of Heraclitus the Ephesian. It is obscure ... But if a μύστης guide you it will be clearer than sunlight." If Heraclitus presented his teaching as a mystery, his Fragment 125 becomes clear: τὰ γὰρ νομιζόμενα κατ' ἀνθρώπους μυστήρια ἀνιερωστὶ μνεῦνται. Why should he refer to the things "called mysteries by men" if he were not contrasting them with true

---

[1]Interesting material on the earlier φυσικοί as mystics, and the bearing of the fact upon Philo's φυσικοὶ ἄνδρες is to be found in Hans Leisegang, "Griechische Philosophie als Mysterion," *Festschrift für Franz Poland (Philogische Wochenschrift*, 1932, nos. 35-38), 245-252. That material is not repeated.

[2]That the ancients regarded Pythagoreanism as a mystery is clear at once from Iamblichus, *Pythag. Vit.*, xxii f., 101-105; xxxii, 226-228.

[3]ix, 16.

mysteries, and if the so-called mysteries were celebrated in an unholy way was
there not in his mind a more correct type of celebration? It is notable also that
in the *Theaetetus* (155e ff.) where Plato expounds some of Heraclitus' doctrines,
he prefaces his exposition with Socrates' warning against letting any of the
uninitiated (ἀμύητοι) hear it, i.e., "those who think nothing exists but what they
can grasp in their two hands." The doctrine itself is stated as the μυστήρια of
certain clever men.[4] It would, then, seem possible that Heraclitus' obscurities
were deliberately designed to keep the true doctrines intelligible only to those
trained in the school to understand them.

Empedocles obviously combined a mystic religion of Orphic base, in which
metempsychosis was the primal belief, with a physical theory of the universe.
He went about proclaiming his philosophy in the guise of a fallen deity among
men who in some way had become "no longer mortal."[5] Were his physical
philosophy and his religion separated by as great a "gulf" as Burnet thinks?[6] Or
did not the saving value of wisdom hinted at in Frag. 132 actually include the
cosmology? "Blessed is the man who has gained the notion of divine wisdom;
wretched he who has a dim notion of the gods in his heart."

In the writings of Plato these possibilities become actualities. "Philosophy
is itself a purification and a way of escape from the 'wheel'," Burnet says of all
Greek thought influenced by Pythagoreanism. But his words and their
implication have been overlooked.[7] The Greek philosophers were scornful of
mystic rites precisely because they believed they had found the true way of
purification in the purgation of the soul by correct teaching. Burnet may be
right that the Pythagoreans gave this mystic meaning to the word philosophy,
but it is demonstrable that philosophy was a means of salvation to Plato, and
that when we get beyond the propaedeutics of the Dialogues the higher ground is
presented as a mystery.

There will never be agreement about the "essential" Plato, any more than
about the "essential" Paul or Jesus, for the simple reason that his writings are so
broadly suggestive that every one can find in them some justification for his
own thought and will inevitably feel that the "essential" element is the one that
appeals to himself. In my opinion, the study of Plato should begin with his
statement in the Seventh Letter that he never put his philosophy into a book,

---

[4]There is to be sure some doubt that 156a ff. describes a doctrine of Heraclitus
himself, though even C. Ritter takes it to be so (*Platon*, II, 97). Taylor's guess
(*Plato*, 330) of Hippasus is attractive. In any case here is a doctrine in which
Heraclitean and Pythagorean elements are mingled and presented as a mystery.
[5]Frag. 112.
[6]*EGP*, 250.
[7]*EGP*, 83.

and had no intention ever of doing so.[8] If this be taken seriously, it is very doubtful whether any of Plato's main arguments represent his objectives. The Dialogues were only propaedeutic, as mathematics itself was a propaedeutic, beyond which philosophy soared into the empyrean in the secret discourses. This position is closely parallel to that of the mysteries in which, similarly, the outsiders, the ἀμύητοι, were in sharp contrast with the μύσται. The question of whether these terms in Plato were intended literally or figuratively turns on the existence not of an initiation rite, but of a belief that the process of learning the higher truths was a real purgation and means of salvation.

Fortunately Plato twice defines a mystery for us. Describing the Orphic mystery, he says that its devotees:

> persuade not only individuals but even cities that there are atonements (λύσεις) and purifications (καθαρμοί) for sins by means of sacrifices and pleasures of sport for those who are yet alive and even for those who are dead. These they call τελετάς which release us from our sins over there (i.e., in Hades), but for those who do not sacrifice terrible things are in store.[9]

This is put into the mouth of Adimantus and doubtless reflects the general notion in Plato's day of the nature and function of at least the Orphic mystery. Again in the *Phaedo,*[10] Socrates, after praising wisdom as the only true objective of man, says that Ultimate Truth (τὸ ἀληθὲς) or true virtue practised with wisdom is a purification from all pleasures and pains.

> And those who founded the mysteries (τελετάς) seem not to be bad fellows at all, but in reality to have long ago hinted that an uninitiated man (ἀμύητοσ καὶ ἀτέλεστος) who comes into Hades would lie in the mud, but that the purified and initiated man (κεκαθαρμένοσ καὶ τετελεσμένοσ) would on his arrival there dwell with the gods. So then there are, as those who have to do with the mysteries (τελετάς) say, "Many who bear the wand, but few Bacchi." These latter are in my opinion none other than those who have rightly pursued philosophy.

Socrates goes on to say that this has been his own aim, and that he would very shortly see, when he reached Hades, whether he had succeeded or not. The passage plainly means that the founders of the mysteries were on the right track when they divided the pure from the impure in the future world, but this purity,

---

[8]*Ep.,* VII, 341c, d. This statement itself had a mystic setting: οὔκουν ἐμόν γε περὶ αὐτῶν ἔστι σύγγραμμα οὐδὲ μήποτε γένηταί ῥητὸν γὰρ οὐδαμῶς ἐστεν ὡς ἄλλα μαθήματα, ἀλλὰ ἐκ πολλῆς συνουσίας γιγνομένης περὶ τὸ πρᾶγμα αὐτὸ καὶ τοῦ συξῆν ἐξαίφνης, οἷον ἀπὸ πυρὸς πηδήσαντος ἐξαφθὲν φῶς, ἐν τῇ ψυχῇ γενόμενον αὐτὸ ἑαυτὸ ἤδη τρέφει.

[9]*Rep,* II, 364e-365a.

[10]69a-d.

as they themselves hinted, was not merely ritualistic, since many performed the rites who were not Bacchi. The true purification was something else, which Socrates identifies with true philosophy. Socrates looks forward quite literally to the testing of his success in after life. He had been practising the true mystery in following philosophy.

This notion is later amplified.[11] "Philosophizing truly" so purifies the soul that it is separated from every bodily contamination, and is judged on its purity in this sense in Hades. Only freedom from bodily nature can prevent the soul from reincarnation, and only philosophy is the true mystery or initiation which can effect such purity: εἰς δέ γε θεῶν γένος μὴ φιλοσοφήσανται καὶ παντελῶς καθαρῷ ἀπιόντι οὐ θέμις ἀφικνεῖσθαι ἀλλ' ἢ τῷ φιλομαθεῖ.[12] So those who want to care properly for their souls devote themselves to the λύσις καὶ καθαρμός of philosophy.[13] This λύσις consists in philosophy's teaching, that reality lies not in things perceived by the senses, but in the invisible things perceived by the soul.[14]

Similar literal statements, that the true philosophy which leads to immaterial reality is the true and only saving mystery, appear elsewhere in Plato's writings. Stesichorus' great speech, which Socrates summarizes in the *Phaedrus,* presents philosophy in exactly the same way. Our fate in successive incarnations is determined entirely by our steadfastness in vision of the immaterial forms. In its original state before incarnation the soul can stay in the blessed fields viewing Reality (τὸ ὄν) along with pure justice, self-control and ἐπιστήμη and sharing in the heavenly feast of ambrosia and nectar.[15] In life the soul's charioteer must control his steeds in order to attain the vision and keep it. Apparently the vision must be seen at least once every thousand years or the soul falls. Once a soul has fallen its only salvation lies in recalling glimpses of truth it had caught in former cycles. It is the function of the philosopher to stimulate memories of this kind and this function is "perfecting oneself in the perfect mysteries" and so "becoming truly τέλεος."[16] In a sense this is only an imitation of the ideal mystery. Plato describes again the rapture of the perfect vision in company with the gods:

> Beauty was a resplendent thing to see at that time when with the blessed chorus we with Zeus and others with another god beheld the blessed sight and spectacle, and were initiated into what it is right to call the most blessed of the mysteries. This mystery we celebrated when we were more

---

[11]*Phaedo,* 80d ff. The more important passages on philosophy as mystery in Plato have recently been brilliantly discussed by Jeanne Croissant, *Aristote et les Mysts,* Liége et Paris, 1983, 159-164.

[12]*Phaedo,* 82c.

[13]*Ibid.,* 82d.

[14]*Ibid.,* 83a-84b; cf. 67c, d.

[15]*Paedrus,* 247c-e. On this Orphic banquet see *Rep,* II, 363c.

[16]*Paedrus,* 249c: τέλεους ἀεὶ τελετὰς τελούμενος.

complete (ὁλόκληρος) and not subject to the evils which have subsequently oppressed us: and we who were initiated into these appearances (φάσματα) which are complete (ὁλόκληρα) simple (ἁπλᾶ), calm (ἀτρεμῆ), and happy, and were given the mystic view (ἐποπτεύοντος) into the pure beam, were pure and unstamped with that thing we now bear about called the body, to which we are bound like an oyster.[17]

Plato goes on to apply this notion to the subject immediately at hand, the power of beauty to awaken the madness of love. The recent initiate into true beauty finds that human loveliness recalls to him a longing for the higher beauty, whereas the uninitiated desires only to possess the beautiful human form. To the initiate, we may therefore infer, love is really a fresh revelation of τὰ ἐποπτικά.[18]

The vision of beauty is presented in exactly the same way in Diotima's speech in the *Symposium*. The first part of her discourse gradually leads to the conclusion that all love, being love of beauty, is really love of immortality, which expresses itself on the bodily plane in the instinct for physical procreation, and has its spiritual counterpart in the desire to beget, with a noble helpmeet, a noble offspring.[19] True love, therefore, is a desire to beget nobility. To have reached this point in the understanding of love is initiation into the lower stages, and this, she says, Socrates could perhaps achieve.[20] But the more advanced degrees of the mystery, τὰ τέλεα καὶ ἐποπτικά, are probably beyond Socrates' power.[21] To enter the higher mystery and come to the "things seen," the aspirant begins as a young man with love for a single beautiful body. Thence he comes to appreciate beautiful bodies in general, and at last to recognize that the beauty in each is a common possession, which leads to an apprehension of the Form of Beauty, and a love for all beautiful bodies. The next step is to recognize that spiritual beauty is higher than bodily beauty, until gradually the expanding mind comes to grasp the common beauty manifest in all sorts of spiritual forms, thoughts and deeds of every kind. This will lead to a vision of the "great sea of beauty" itself, the Form of Beauty in a sense much clearer and more accurate than the form previously inferred from beautiful bodies. Previous labor had been directed to this single end, the vision of Beauty itself which is unchanging, pure, unmixed and perfect, and of which beautiful objects, bodies, or thoughts, only in a sense partake. For a person who has achieved this

---

[17]*Ibid.*, 250b, c. This last figure was in Philo's mind when he said that at his death Moses "cast off his body which grew around him like the shell of an oyster, while his soul which was thus laid bare desired its migration thence"; *Virt*, 76. See my *By Light, Light*, 197.

[18]*Paedrus*, 250d-253.

[19]On love as desire for immortality see especially *Symp*, 206d, e; 207c.

[20]ταῦτα τὰ ἐρωτικὰ ἴσως, ὦ Σώκρατες, κἂν σὺ μυηθείης *Symp*, 209e.

[21]*Symp*, 210a. This is of course Socrates' modesty, to suggest the great superiority of Diotima.

vision, an evil life (φαῦλος βίος) is no longer possible.[22] Here again the vision of the forms, to which true philosophy alone can lead one, is the supreme, the only saving mystery. As the only real mystery it is the literal mystery.

The line of ascent to the mystic ἐποπτικά in the Symposium at once suggests the passage which is probably closer to the Lecture on the Good than anything Plato published: the description of the Dialectical Ladder, and its counterpart the Myth of the Cave, in the *Republic*.[23] Throughout both these descriptions it is clear that the objective is to raise the soul to a vision of the forms, and, supremely, of the Good. Mathematics is introduced as the best preliminary discipline for this process, but, as it represents the realm of διάνοια rather than of νοῦς or ἐπιστήμη, it is only a preliminary. There is no indication whatever, here or elsewhere, that Plato did more than approach the τελευτή by means of mathematical analogies intelligible only to the mathematician, but valuable for philosophy as a means rather than an end. Mystical terms are not elaborated in the passage, but appear inevitably when Plato describes the ultimate achievement, the τελευτᾷ εἰς εἴδη, the coming ἐπὶ τελευτήν.[24]

Plato begins this discussion with the fact that the Good was to the conceptual world what the sun is to the visible world,[25] and he returns to this figure in the Myth of the Cave, the Orphic pattern of which has long been recognized. Here escape from the lower world is exactly as in the earlier Dialogues, an emergence from our world of appearance to a final vision of the forms of reality, with their supreme form, the Good. The whole is obviously a description of the "true philosophy" which was the "true mystery," as indeed the *Republic* itself is a passionate attempt to demonstrate that the state can only be saved by citizens trained to see the Realities, and hence competent to direct the lives of others toward what is real and true. It is no figure of speech that Philosophy purifies men's souls and makes them ready for this world and the next. To Plato there was no other escape from the wheel.

In view of the agreement of these passages, and of Plato's statement that his true philosophy is not elaborated in any Dialogue, because it is "unutterable," it seems to me that the bulk of his writings must be understood as propaedeutic. Problem after problem can be posed and left unsolved because the reader is not ready for the solution. It is enough for the Dialogue to stimulate thought, shake confidence in clichés, and drive the reader to the Academy for initiation into the

---

[22]*Symp*, 210a-212a.
[23]This is clearly pointed out by Croissant, pp. 159 ff.
[24]*Rep*, 511b, c.
[25]*Rep*, 508b ff.

truth.[26] Plato often scorns the mysteries about him (though he draws heavily upon Orphic sources) because he knew that the frenzied dancing of bacchanals,[27] for example, falls pathetically short of accomplishing its objective.

It is clear that Platonism was later presented as the perfect mystery. In the *Epinomis* (986a-d) initiation into the "stars" is said to give immortality, knowledge and virtue.[28] In his earlier period, while still under Platonic influence, Aristotle in all probability spoke the same language. J. Croissant's recent and brilliant study, to which reference has already been made, has thrown much new light upon the attitude of Aristotle to mystery. Approaching Aristotle in the way Jaeger has now made inevitable, Croissant first analyzes Aristotle's attitude toward the popular mystery religions and shows that Aristotle's aesthetic κάθαρσις is opposed to the mystic notion; although it began as mysticism it changed into an elaborate rationalization of the experience in terms of medical theory. He then shows how Aristotle similarly began with the view that the goal of philosophy is initiation, a mystic vision which was explicitly made the true initiation and mystery, but replaced Plato's Idea of the Good with the higher νοῦς of man himself, as the source of that illumination which was the object of philosophy.[29] The materials Croissant has gathered are so extensive and so thoroughly analyzed that it would be useless to repeat them. One thing, however, stands out in striking relief: that Aristotle's successors in Hellenistic and Roman times did not lose sight of the fact that he, like Plato, had presented the goal of philosophy as an initiation into Truth, and it is owing to their quotations that we know this phase of Aristotle's development at all. To them Aristotle was like Plato in making Philosophy into the true mystery. One of Croissant's quotations from Plutarch is well worth repeating:

Knowledge of that which is νοητός, pure, and simple, flashing through the soul like lightning, at a stroke (ἅπαξ) gives one power to attain

---

[26]This relation of the ordinary detail of a Dialogue to the real objective of philosophy appears in passing in *Gorg*, 497c. Here Callicles resents Socrates pushing him with "trifling" questions. He wants to get on to more important matters. Socrates says that Callicles desires to be initiated into the higher mysteries without first being initiated into the lower; and Socrates keeps Callicles to the lower, as Plato keeps his readers in general, because he knows that Callicles, like all men, must begin at the bottom.

[27]*Laws*, 815c. On Plato's attitude to the popular mysteries see Croissant, 13-20, 53 ff.

[28]See the *Introduction* of Albinus (2nd Cent. A.D.) to the writings of Plato, §4 f. (C.F. Hermann, *Appendix Platonica*, Leipz. 1875, 149). The attempt is made to schematize the dialogues from the first stages of refutation up to the full attainment of virtue and thence to mystic vision. αὐτῇ τῇ περὶ τὴν φύσιν ἱστορίᾳ ἐντυγχάνοντες καὶ τῇ λεγομένῃ θεολογίᾳ καὶ τῇ τῶν ὅλων διατάξει ἀντοψόμεθα τὰ θεῖα ἐναργῶς.

[29]But even at the end the saving power of θεωρία in the Nicomachean Ethics is clearly recognizable. See W. Jaeger, *Aristotles*, 100 ff., 164-170.

(θιγεῖν) and to behold (προοιδεῖν). Wherefore Plato and Aristotle call this part of philosophy the ἐποπτικόν, when those who have by reason gone beyond objects of opinion, mixed and variform, come to that [Existence] which is simple and immaterial, and in a sense attain unto the pure truth concerning it; this is the goal (τέλος), they think, of perfect (ἐντελής) philosophy.[30]

Philo is directly in line with this tradition, and the Old Testament was for him a guide to the true philosophy by which man was thought saved by association with the immaterial.[31] If only this side of Philo was represented the question whether mystic Judaism was really a mystery could be answered in only one way. It was, like Platonism, a true mystery because it was the only way man could achieve salvation from the flesh.[32]

But there is another side to Philo's Mystery, as there was another side to Plutarch's mystic thought. From Plato and Aristotle to Plutarch and on to the Neo-Platonists the great religious achievement was the development of the Hellenistic conception of a sacrament. Some men, like Plotinus, could keep to pure mystery in the philosophic sense and seed τὰ ἐποπτικά only by philosophic means. Others, of whom Plutarch is our best example, developed a sacramental notion in which the Platonic kind of mystery was combined with the popular mystic rites. Plutarch practised and admired these not because they were effective in themselves, though like any good sacramentarian he apparently had a deep respect for the *opus operatum*. The real meaning of the ritual act was that it supplied a revelation of truth. The act, like the myth, had value because it led men into the mystery of immaterial reality in the Platonic sense. From this time on men wanted both a ritual act and a mystic philosophy. The act, for the more perceptive members of the group, was a visible sign of invisible grace; the real mystic experience was essentially not in the visible sign but in the invisible apprehension.

---

[30]Plutarch, *De Iside et Osiride*, 77.

[31]This is the thesis of my *By Light, Light*.

[32]A most interesting passage in Clement of Alexandria (*Stromata*, I, 176, 1 f.) is mentioned by H.G. Marsh, "The Use of μυστήριον in the Writings of Clement of Alexandria," *Journal of Theol. Stud*, XXXVII (1936), 68. Clement says that the philosophy of Moses is divided into four parts, the historical, the legislative, the sacerdotal (ὅ ἐστιν τῆς φυσικῆς θεωρίας), and the theological, which is ἡ ἐποπτεία, ἥν φησιν ὁ Πλάτων τῶν μεγάλων ὄντως εἶναι μυστηρίων, but which Aristotle called metaphysics. Clement certainly has this from Philo or another mystic Jew. The passage illustrates beautifully how the Jewish Mystery was oriented by the Jews themselves with Platonic philosophy as mystery. After this essay was in print there appeared Hans von Balthasar's, "Le Mysterion d'Origine," *Recherches de Science Religieuse*, XXVI (1936), 513-562; XXVII (1937), 38-64. It is a most illuminating sequel to this study for Christian thought. He is discussing "cet intellectualisme alexandrin, pour qui le myst ne serait qu'une sorte de second lettre derri le premi, dont elle ne se distinguerait pas qualitativement."

It is obvious that the Jews of Philo's period took a similar view of Jewish rites. I have already shown elsewhere how every detail of the Jerusalem cultus, the temple and its rites, the vestments, victims,[33] and the rest, were allegorized exactly as Plutarch allegorized the rites and robes of Isis and Osiris to show that sharing in the rites was to share in a sacrament which brought to men a mystic salvation.[34] Philo did not by any means stop with this. The whole body of ritual laws is similarly allegorized, so that the Jew could feel that each command disclosed a saving revelation of truth in the mystic sense, a saving identification of himself with immaterial reality. Circumcision is valuable in God's sight, Philo explains, for several reasons, but chiefly because it "drives πονρὰ δόξα from the soul, and all other things which are not φιλόθεοι."[35] It is an outward sign of inward κάθαρσις, an inner experience not in the sense of Jeremiah, but in that of Plato and the mysteries.

The sacrifices in the temple are all mystic rites for Philo. The animals and priests alike must be flawless in body as a symbol of the flawless soul offered to God.[36] The twelve loaves of showbread symbolize the twelve months of the year in which nature accomplishes its circuit. Bread is used, in contrast to delicacies, because it represents the chief of virtues, ἐγκράτεια.[37] The bread is accompanied by frankincense and salt which are likewise symbolic. The spectacle of the altar containing these simple things appears ridiculous to people who think in terms of costly banquets, he says, but have a quite different meaning to those who have learned to live in a way pleasing to God, i.e., to those "who have learned to belittle the pleasures of the flesh, and who, disciplining themselves in θεωρία of the things in nature, have a share in the pleasures and enjoyments of the mind."[38]

The festivals are similarly interpreted as mystic rites. Philo schematizes them so that there shall be the perfect mystic number ten. The first festival is the "feast of every day," a festival in which man so rises by contemplation that he, while fixed on earth with his body, is in his winged mind a genuine part of the great cosmic cycle, until he finds his joy τῷ καλῷ δι' αὐτὸ τὸ καλόν which he regards as the only ἀγαθόν. Joy in its fullest sense is possible only to the supreme Good, which is God, but the true mystic can come in a sense to share it.[39] This is the universal festival, the feast of every day, and is obviously a later version of the philosophic mystery of Plato. The Sabbath, the second

---

[33]On victims see *Spec*, i, 162 ff. References to Philo are by the section divisions of Cohn-Wendland. Titles are abbreviated according to the scheme published in *By Light, Light*, pp. xiii f.

[34]See my *By Light, Light*, chap. IV.

[35]*Spec.*, i, 4-12.

[36]*Spec*, i, 166 ff.

[37]*Ibid.*, 172 ff.

[38]*Ibid.*, 175 f.

[39]*Spec.* ii, 41-55.

festival, has not only the physical value of a day of rest, but is important because by the rest of the body the soul is liberated for the θεωρητικὸς βίος.[40] The New Moon, the third festival, is praised largely in astronomical terms. Behind what Philo says apparently lies reference to the Cosmic Mystery, but he section is not specific.[41] The fourth, the festival of the Passover, makes of every man a priest, and the people who look beyond the letter by allegory, that is Jews who follow the Mystery, see in the feast the celebration or symbol of the great migration from body to spirit, the ψυχῆς κάθαρσις practised by every σοφίας ἐραστής.[42] The Passover was certainly elaborated in more detailed allegory for the significance of each part of its ritual to mystics, for in one passage Philo says:

> So then let us always be well girded and entirely ready, renouncing all delay, for thanksgiving (εὐχαριστία)[43] and honor of the Almighty. For we are bidden to keep the Passover, which is the passage from the life of the passions to the practice of virtue, "with our loins girded," ready for service. We must grip the material body of flesh, that is "the sandals" with "our feet" that stand firm and secure. We must bear "in our hands the staff" of education (παιδεία) to the end that we may walk straight and without stumbling through all the affairs of life. Last of all we must eat our meal "in haste," since it is not a mortal passing over, for it is called the πάσχα of God who is without beginning or end. And rightly is it so called, since nothing is beautiful which is not of God and divine.[44]

In discussing the Unleavened Bread of the fifth festival Philo calls it "the clearest symbol (δεῖγμα) of the unmixed food (ἀμιγὴς τροφή)" which is prepared by φύσις.[45] The sixth festival, that of the dedication of the Sheaf, leads Philo into a long digression on the notion that the Jewish nation is, as a group, a nation of priests for the whole world. As they have been purified by οἱ ἀγνευτικοὶ καθάρσιοι, the study and discipline of the Law, so in this feast they make an offering for the whole world. What they offer is a consecration to φύσις (here, as frequently in Philo, God) of her products, the supreme εὐχάριστος so that man can thereafter use the fruits of the soil without sin

---

[40]Ibid., 56-70.
[41]Ibid., 140-144.
[42]Ibid., 145-149.
[43]In Migr, 25 the Passover is ἡ πρὸς τὸν σωτῆρα θεὸν εὐχαριστία.
[44]Sacr, 63; cf. Congr, 106; LA, iii, 94; Heres, 255. In LA, iii, 165 the "step forward" is the πρόβατον, the Paschal lamb.
[45]Spec, ii, 150-161, especially 161. In Congr, 161-168 the unleavened bread is elaborately allegorized. It is ἱερόν, and its nourishment inspires φιλία τοῦ καλοῦ; it is a feeding on τὰ παιδείας δόγματα

(ἀνυπαίτιον).[46] In spite of the general lack of "allegory" in the sense of mystic interpretation in the *Exposition,* a single sentence in the explanation of the seventh festival, that of First Fruits, lifts us to a glimpse of what the offering meant for mystics. In this case, Philo says, the First Fruits is offered in the form of a leavened cake or loaf which is "a material (αἰσθητής) εὐχαριστία by means of leavened loaves of the invisible εὐπάθεια in our mind (διάνοια)." This comes very close indeed to the "visible sign of an invisible grace." In a more mystic writing this must have been much expanded,[47] and in *de Sacrif. Ab. et Caini* 52-87, a long allegory is evolved, based upon the contrast between Cain's offering and the true offering of "First Fruits," with which the "buried cakes" of Sarah are associated. The feast of First Fruits, with its bread, is obviously at the background of the whole passage, one of the most mystical in Philo. Sarah's cakes are "buried" (one of the inmost secrets of the Mystery) because they are the food of the Mystic Three. Various other sacred meals, including manna, are also included in the discussion, which seems entirely to have forgotten its starting point and objective until Philo suddenly concludes that all this is the true First Fruits. I suspect that the passage is purposely made almost unintelligible lest it fall into the hands of the uninitiated, for every comer, he says (§ 60), may not understand the θεῖα ὄργια, the divine rites. These rites seem to be the mystic explanation of the Jewish festivals. Here the bread seems a sacrament of complete dedication, spiritual food, given to one who has abandoned the body and dedicated the perfect "First Fruit," his own ψυχή.

The eighth festival, which Philo calls that of the "Sacred Month," is the New Year. In this Philo is chiefly concerned with the ceremony of the Trumpet, the Shofar, so frequent in Jewish inscriptions. To him the whole festival parallels closely the ἱερομηνία of the Greeks, the period of armistice which was proclaimed among the Greeks for the sacred games.[48] So the trumpet, ordinarily a signal for war, in the festival proclaims cosmic peace. In the more allegorical interpretation, the "trumpet of peace in the soul torn by conflict" was the Logos, we learn from the Pseudo-Justinian *Oratio.*[49]

The Festival of the Fast (Day of Atonement) is the ninth festival. It is celebrated as a fast in order to turn men from the material to the immaterial. The

---

[46]*Spec,* ii, 162-175. In *ibid.,* i, 270-272 he similarly makes the perfect sacrifice a εὐχαριστία. A man must come to the sacrifice pure in body, and purified in soul by σοφία καὶ τὰ σοφίας δόγματα as well as by the other virtues. Then his true sacrifice will be the offering of himself, singing hymns aloud, to be sure, but giving the true εὐχαριστία by projecting his νοητά to God alone. In *ibid.,* 286-288 the fire unextinguished on the altar represents the εὐχαριστία, the perfect sacrifice, in the heart; it also represents the φῶς διανοίας, divine σοφία or ἐπιστήμη, leading the soul to θεωρία τῶν ἀσωμάτων καὶ νοητῶν.

[47]*Spec,* ii, 176-187. Mystic numerology is also connected with the feast.

[48]See Heinemann in L. Cohn, *Die Werke Philos ... in deutscher Ueberset,* II, 159, n. 4.

[49]*Spec,* ii, 188-192. See *By Light, Light,* 303.

transitory can never truly nourish. In the absence of ordinary food God fed the fathers with manna from heaven, instead of unspiritual (ἄψυχος) food.[50] So men are turned from the things ministered (τὰ χορηγούμενα) to the one who ministers (χορηγός) in exalted worship. This festival is certainly a mystic sacrament for Philo. It is celebrated on the tenth of the month to bring in the mystic associations of the perfect number ten. The hierophant (Moses) has established the fast on the tenth not to lead us into bodily hunger, but enable the shining (or translucent, διαυγές) and pure (καθαρόν) dampness which comes from the λογικὴ πηγή to be borne into the soul, so that the soul can feast itself on "the things really worthy of being seen and heard (τὰ θέας καὶ ἀκιῆς ἄξια)", i.e., clearly, on the true mystic ἐποπτικά and teachings.[51]

The tenth festival is that of the Tabernacles. It is celebrated in the early autumn, just before the Jewish New Year, and so is the culminating feast of the year. By numerology it is made to represent the achievement of all that has been attempted in the early festivals, the final passing over from the boundary of the material to the immaterial. The text is too corrupt for satisfactory rendering, but its purport is clear.[52]

At the end Philo briefly summarizes. All the festivals have sprung from a common mother, the number seven, and minister to bodies by giving them a splendid regimen (ἀβροδίαιτος); the festivals minister to souls by philosophy.[53]

What is this philosophic doctrine of the festivals or Jewish ὄργια?[54] We are beginning to see that the true celebration of a festival was its use as a sacrament, a step from the material to the immaterial life and being of God. In one passage in the *Allegorical Writings* Philo begins specifically to answer the question: what is the God-given principle (δόγμα) of the festivals for the mystic associates of philosophy (οἱ φιλοσοφίας θιασῶται);[55] but he is led into a digression from which he never extricates himself. He begins:

---

[50]Manna is abundantly cited as a symbol of mystical food: see *By Light, Light*, 208.

[51]*Spec*, ii, 183-203; esp. 199-202.

[52]*Ibid.*, 204-213; esp. 212.

[53]*Ibid.*, 214.

[54]In *Spec*, i, 269 Philo indicates, what is to be suspected, that the allegory of rites in this, a part of the *Exposition*, is only a superficial treatment. Another treatise contained the full allegory. Whether that "other treatise" was the lost part of the *Questiones* or not, a natural assumption, it is clear that much as is here, Philo's real understanding of the ritual was still more allegorical, and presumably more mystical, than what we now have. On the fact that the *Exposition*, a series of works designed for proselytes, is highly restricted in allegory, see my "Philo's Exposition of the Law and His De Vita Mosis," *HTR*, XXVII (1933), 109-125.

[55]*Cher*, 85 ff.

> The δόγμα is this: God alone in the true sense keeps a festival. Joy and gladness and rejoicing are His alone; to Him alone it is given to enjoy the peace which has not element of war [this is the New Year's Trumpet].[56]

So Philo goes on to a long description of God in His perfection of nature and happiness. We are reminded that the *Phaedrus* the only true mystery was that of the heavens in which the gods participated. In contrast to this festival of God Philo describes at length the sinfulness of pagan festivals which seem devoted entirely to fleshly riotings. The Jewish festival, we are left to infer, is an imitation of the true festival of God, not a sharing in human and material nature, but a transition, as far as man can go, to the realm of divine existence.[57]

Philo does not discuss any special meal which was the "sacred table or food" of the ἀληθεῖς τελεταί,[58] that food to which those unpurified must not be admitted, but he might have said it, apparently, of the Passover, of the Unleavened Bread, or of any Jewish festival, so truly has he made the festivals into mystic sacraments. That mystic Jews had a special rite of initiation is not apparent in our evidence, but that they formed special groups for celebrating the Jewish "sacraments" in their own way with their own explanations and comments seems almost inevitable from what Philo says.

It has appeared that the mystic Jew saw the supreme revelation of saving truth in his Torah, when properly understood by allegory, and felt that because he had unique access to and revelation of the immaterial world, he had the true Mystery, αἱ ἀληθεῖς τελεταί. He had the true Mystery in the Platonic sense, the truly saving philosophy of the purely Good and Beautiful, and he had it also in the sense that he, and he alone, had the divine ὄργια, the right celebration of which meant coming into the fellowship and joy of the immaterial reality of God Himself. However we may now want to use the term, the mystic Jew himself gloried in the fact that his was not only a "real" mystery, but the only real one.

---

[56]*Ibid.*, 86.

[57]A similar idea is developed in *Spec*, i, 193. In contrast to heathen riots God summons the Jews to their festivals first with the command that they "go into the sanctuary to share in the hymns, prayers, and sacrifices in such a way that both from the place and from the things they see (ὁρώμενα) and hear ... they may come to love ἐγκράτεια and εὐσέβεια"; and thirdly that they may be warned from sinning by the sacrifice for sin, for, while a man seeks λύσις from sins he will hardly be planning new offences. The ὁρώμενα καὶ λεγόμενα as well as the λύσις, show at once that to Philo the temple service was a mystic rite.

[58]*By Light, Light*, 260 f.

Chapter Five

Philo's Exposition of the Law and his *De vita Mosis*

Harvard Theological Review 1933, 27:109-125

The problem of Philo's Exposition of the Law and of its relation to the treatise De vita Mosis has, it seems to me, not yet been solved.

The Exposition is one of Philo's three great series of commentaries on the Pentateuch. It comprised originally De opificio mundi, De Abrahamo, De Isaaco, De Iacobo, De Josepho, De decalogo, De specialibus legibus, De virtutibus, and De praemiis et poenis, of which all are preserved but De Isaaco and De Iacobo. In contrast with the two great series called the Allegory of the Sacred Laws and the Quaestiones, the Exposition goes much less into allegory, and tells the biblical stores in extensive narrative, quoting the laws in detail in a way not attempted by the other two. That the Allegory and the Quaestiones were designed for thoughtful Jews has never been, and never could be, doubted. About the Exposition opinion has been more diverse, but since the discussion by Massebieau (1889) there has been unanimity in regarding it too as designed for Jews.

The treatise De vita Mosis has for nearly a century been classed in a group of miscellaneous writings, with various apologetic arguments and all addressed to gentiles. The De vita Mosis is different from Philo's other apologies – the fragmentary Hypothetica, Adversus Flaccum, and the Legatio – in its complete unconcern about refuting attacks against the Jews, and in being, rather than a polemic, an elementary introduction to the ideals of Judaism for interested outsiders through the story of Moses and of the establishment of the Jewish Law. It is different also in that it is referred to in the Exposition as representing an integral part of the argument of the Exposition. For our purpose we may begin with these latter references, which do not seem to have been adequately appraised.

Leopold Cohn said of one of these: "Wenn im Anfang von *de caritate* auf die *Vita Mosis* hingewiesen ist, so spricht die dabei beobachtete genaue Art des Citierens gerade dafür, dass es sich um ein selbständiges und nicht derselben

Schriftenreihe angehöriges Werk handelt."[1] The passage to which Cohn referred
would at first sight bear him out; it is printed in his subsequent edition in De
virtutibus 52:

> Formerly, in a work of two books which I wrote on the Life of Moses, I
> described Moses' deeds from infancy to old age with respect to his care
> for and supervision of each individual and all men. But it is worthwhile
> to mention one or two things which he set in order at the time of his
> death.

Philo then goes on to tell the story of the appointment of Joshua as the new
leader and of the death of Moses, not as a review of something already told in De
vita Mosis but as a supplement to that work. Cohn is quite right in concluding
that De vita Mosis is assumed to be a treatise independent of the Exposition, but
he misses the fact that there is sufficient connection between the two so that
Philo could assume that the reader of the Exposition would already have read the
other, and hence needed merely to be provided with a supplement to the account
of Moses' life in the earlier work. The Exposition makes no such assumption
about any of Philo's other writings, and it seems natural to conclude that the two
were in some sense companion pieces, like Luke's Gospel and the Acts, in
which the earlier work was independent, yet is assumed in the later work to have
been read. Further Cohn does not mention the fact that in De praemiis et poenis
53 ff., in a summary of the course of the entire argument of the Exposition, the
points of De vita Mosis are given as essential links in the chain of thought, but
no similar account is included of any other of Philo's treatises.

Wendland[2] discussed the passage from De caritate, ch. 1, and agrees with
Cohn that De caritate did not belong to De vita Mosis, but was a part of the De
virtutibus and so of the Exposition. In a note he parallels this passage with the
reference in De praemiis et poenis 53 ff. in order to show that neither reference
implies that the treatise in which it is found is a part of De vita Mosis rather
than of the Exposition. Cohn and Wendland were both arguing against the
position of Massebieau,[3] who inferred from the references to De vita Mosis and
from the general character of the works that De caritate, the lost De pietate,[4] De

---

[1]"Einteilung und Chronologie der Schriften Philos," in *Philologus,* VII,
Supplementband, 1899, p. 417.
[2]"Philo und Clemens Alexandrinus," in *Hermes,* XXXI, 1896, pp. 435-443,
especially pp. 440 f.
[3]"Le Classement des Oeuvres de Philon," in *Bibliotèque de l'École des Hautes
Études,* Sciences Religieuses, Paris, I, 1889, pp. 42 ff.
[4]On the whole Schürer's argument seems to me more convincing against the
inclusion of De pietate than Wendland and Cohn's in its favor. In the absence of
the work itself there is little more to be said on either side. See Schürer,
Geschichte des judischen Volkes im Zeitalter Jesu Christi, 4th ed., 1909, p. 671,
notes 99-101, and the references there to Cohn and Wendland.

humanitate, and De paenitentia could not be parts of the Exposition (De virtutibus), but are "dependencies" of De vita Mosis. Cohn's and Wendland's arguments are entirely convincing insofar as they show that these treatises must have been parts of the Exposition. But the fact remains that in tone and style these treatises are markedly like De vita Mosis, and neither Cohn nor Wendland explains why in the Exposition, which they consider designed for Jewish readers, De vita Mosis alone of all Philo's writings is treated as an integral part of the argument.

De vita Mosis itself has a passage which is germane in this connection. Philo says of the Pentateuch:

> These [the books of Moses] comprise on the one hand the historical part on the other the part which deals with the commands and prohibitions, to which we shall come secondly, after we have first analyzed the part which stands first in order. The historical part is itself composed of the portion which treats of the creation and the genealogical portion. The genealogical portion in turn is composed of two sections dealing respectively with the punishment of the wicked and the honor destined for the righteous. But it must be explained why Moses began the law-book as he did and put the statement of the commands and prohibitions in the second place (ii. 45-47 [ch. 81]).

The discussion that follows is concerned with answering the question raised in the last sentence, namely why the legislation should have been preceded by the historical section. Moses did not write history, Philo explains, for the entertainment of his readers. The historical section was included to show that the author of the laws was the God of nature and that he who obeys the laws is following the nature of the universe (ii. 48). He then speaks, briefly and generally, of the fact that the individual laws are copies of the eternal universal patterns, and goes into more detail to show that nature sanctions the Jewish Law by rewarding the virtuous and punishing the wicked. The case of Noah and his generation is discussed at some length as an illustration of this sanction of the Law by nature, and then we come to the sudden break at which the second book of the treatise in Mangey's edition ends. That is to say, of the discussion proposed in the sentences quoted Philo has dealt only with the general introductory problem stated at the end of the above quotation, namely why the historical part should have been put before the laws, with a brief treatment of nature's sanction of the Law. The definite promise to analyze (ἀκριβοῦν) the historical part and then as a sequal (δεύτερον) go on and discuss the specific laws, is not fulfilled in De vita Mosis.

Schürer speaks of the passage from De vita Mosis.[5] Massebieau had recognized that Philo cannot possibly have accomplished the proposed discussion

---

[5]*Geschichte des jüdischen Volkes im Zeitalter Jesu Christi,* 4th ed., 1909, III, p. 675.

without considerable space, and consequently he supposes a very large section to
have been lost at the point which Mangey adopted as the end of Book ii. But
Massebieau admits that De vita Mosis must originally have comprised two
books only, as is proved by both internal and external evidence; and Schürer
rightly felt that this necessarily shows the lost section to have been limited in
extent. Hence Schürer is forced to hold that a long section would not have been
needed to cover the ground proposed. But that cannot be admitted. Philo has
promised a detailed analysis of the entire Pentateuch, and this would certainly
require very considerable space. Such an extended discussion of the Law is
incompatible with the structure of De vita Mosis. What neither Massebieau nor
Schürer recognized is that the plan proposed by Philo in De vita Mosis for his
analysis of the Pentateuch is exactly the plan of the Exposition – in substance,
purpose, and method. The matter would become simple if we were to assume
that in the lost section, which then may well have been brief, Philo referred his
readers to a companion document which he was about to write or was in the
course of writing,[6] namely the Exposition. In any case the fact remains that in
De vita Mosis Philo promises to make an analysis of the Pentateuch of a kind
which he actually accomplished in the Exposition.

The references, then, in De caritate, De praemiis et poenis, and De vita
Mosis itself are best satisfied by supposing that De vita Mosis and the
Exposition, while independent writings, were companion pieces.

An obstacle to such a conclusion is the general agreement of scholars that
while De vita Mosis is a missionary and propaganda document designed for
gentiles, the Exposition is written as a less technical presentation of Judaism
than the Allegory, and designed for a less esoteric circle of Jews, but still
definitely for Jews. If the two documents were thus written with different
purposes and for different audiences, they can hardly have been companion
pieces.

Schürer, in the second edition of his *History* (1886),[7] is the last important
scholar, so far as I know, to state explicitly that the Exposition was designed for
non-Jews, and to insist upon a close similarity of literary character between it
and De vita Mosis. Massebieau's differing view[8] rests primarily on "l'impression
générale" which the Exposition made upon him; but he gave a few passages as
samples of the sort of statement which had led him to infer that Philo was

---

[6]According as we assume De vita Mosis ii. 115 to contain a reference to De
opificio mundi or to another treatise now lost.
[7]As represented in the English translation, *A History of the Jewish People*, 1886,
II, iii, pp. 338 and 348 f. Schürer's later change of view is mentioned in his
candid and appreciative review of Massebieau in *Theologische Literaturzeitung*,
1891, cols. 91-96. H. Leisegang, in *Die Religion in Geschichte und Gegenwart*,
IV, 1930, col. 1196, merely states that the Exposition, as compared with the
Allegory, is designed for a larger circle of readers, including non-Jews.
[8]"Le Classement des Oeuvres de Philon," p. 38, n. 3.

writing for Jews, with the warning: "Les quelques citations que je vais faire ne peuvent remplacer l'impression générale que cause la lecture de cette section." These citations must be examined. I give them according to the older enumeration he used, adding that of Cohn and Wendland's edition.

1. Dec. orac. 1 (De decalogo 1). Massebieau thinks that Philo's phrase τοῦ ἡμετέρου ἔθνους implies that the reader is also Jewish. But such a use of an editorial first person plural does not at all imply that the reader is included. It is a frequent and natural usage to speak of "our" trade or "our" family in contrast to "yours," and nothing in the passages prevents such an interpretation here.

2. Mon. i. 7 (De specialibus legibus i. 51-55). Massebieau feels that the exhortation "a chatier les Juifs apostate" implies a Jewish reader. But a direct exhortation to Jews is not given; Philo only says, "It is a good thing to charge all who are zealous for the truth" to smite the apostate. Indeed, in the first half of this very section the reader appears conceived far rather as gentile than as Jew. Proselytes are effusively praised as equal to those Jews who were loyal to their God-given εὐγένεια, and as worthy of receiving an equal place in all the rights and privileges of the chosen race. In contrast to both Jews and proselytes are the apostate Jews, in punishing whom "all who are zealous for the truth," that is, as the context shows, Jews and pious gentiles alike, should unite. To say the least, there is nothing here to mark the passage as designed especially for Jewish readers.

3. De praem. sacerdotum 5 (De specialibus legibus i. 153). Here, as in No. 1, the first person plural is used, and need not be taken to include the reader.

4. De sacrific. 10 (De specialibus legibus i. 314). Of this the same is to be said. The prosperity of the wicked, says Philo, is a temptation to "us" who have been bred in the true law and piety. It is notable that this statement follows again one of Philo's most ingratiating passages about proselytes (308-313).

5. The last two passages which Massebieau adduces, De septen. 9 (De specialibus legibus ii. 79 ff.) and De spec. leg. iii. 5 (De specialibus legibus iii. 29), are both addressed to a Jew direct. But both are not addressed by Philo to his own reader, but are reproductions of what Moses is supposed to have declared to the Jewish reader of the Law, and both are introduced by φησί to indicate that it is Moses that is speaking. Both passages are indeed addresses to a Jew, but they are imaginary quotations from Moses, given here for the benefit of any reader whether Jew or gentile.

"Je pourrais continuer," says Massebieau. "Il fallait montrer au moins par quelques citations que M. Schürer n'a pas eu raison de dire que *l'exposition de la loi* s'addressait a des 'non-juifs'."

It is unfortunate that Massebieau did not give further examples, for the passages he gives do not at all justify his impression of the Exposition as a whole. On the other side, his position is still further weakened by the fact that the four treatises which he regarded as "dependencies" of De vita Mosis, and hence suitable for an address to gentiles, have been provided to be parts of the Exposition. Yet other scholars, like Cohn,[9] have simply accepted Massebieau's argument as conclusive without supplementing it. Even Schürer in his third (1898) and fourth edition modified the reference to "non-Jews," and merely says that the Exposition is intended "einem glichst weiten Kreise von Lesern," referring to Massebieau without further comment. Yet he insisted no less emphatically than before that De vita Mosis is in its entire literary character closely related to the Exposition. "As in the larger work the Mosaic legislation is expounded, so are here the life and work of the legislator himself." So far as the literary character of De vita Mosis is concerned, he says in another passage, it would be adapted for a place in the group of treatises which make up the Exposition.[10]

Schürer was unquestionably right about the literary congeniality of the two treatises, and yet he, with all other Philonic scholars, seems to have been affected by Massebieau's "impression générale." Against Massebieau one can show, as has been seen, that his passages do not justify him, but no specific passages seem to indicate definitely that Philo was addressing gentiles. But a general impression is much better founded on general characteristics than on dubious proof-texts, and some of these general characteristics, particularly in contrast to the works we know as designed for Jews, may now be mentioned.

(1) In the Exposition, especially in De Josepho, Joseph, as a politician analogous to the Roman rule of Egypt, is a highly admirable being, almost one of the νόμοι ἔμψυχοι, though distinctly lower than the patriarchs; in the Allegory several passages, but most extensively one in the second book of De somniis, depict Joseph still as a politician analogous to the Roman prefect, but as a despicable creature, a threat to all that is noble in Judaism or in nature. Massebieau and Bréhier[11] have recognized that Philo's attitude toward political life was different in different treatises, and have constructed a remarkable imaginary series of persecutions of the Jews to account for Philo's vacillations. When all was at peace, they explain, Philo wrote scornfully but tolerantly of the practical life of the politician; when times were bad, he regarded political activity as an evil necessity, or recommended shrinking from public life into complete asceticism. On this basis they try to date the works of Philo. It seems never to have occurred to them to try to account for Philo's differences in tone and attitude by a difference of audience addressed, or by a chronic vacillation in Philo's own temperament, or by both together. Schürer was right in rejecting Massebieau's and Bréhier's chronological constructions as fantastic, but he offered no

---

[9]"Einteilung und Chronologie der Schriften Philos," p. 415, and *Die Werke Philos von Alexandria in deutscher Übersetzung*, I, 219.

[10]Schürer, 3rd ed., III, pp. 511, 515, and 523 f.; 4th ed., III, pp. 659, 666, and 675.

[11]"Chronologie de la Vie et des Oeuvres de Philon," in *Revue de l'histoire des Religions*, LIII, 1906, pp. 25-64, 164-185, 267-289.

explanation of Philo's variations to take its place. My own suggestion for a solution can be briefly stated as follows. The contrast between the politician of De Josepho and of De somniis seems easily explained if the Exposition be taken as addressed to gentiles interested in Judaism as a religion but retaining their gentile political point of view, while the Allegory, being addressed to Jews, can express, in a veiled form to be sure, the Jews' secret hatred of Roman domination. The passage in De specialibus legibus ii. 1 ff. is not due to a reaction against Roman rule, but reflects an inner conflict in Philo between his own natural political interest and obligation and a theoretical ascetic rejection of worldly concerns. Into this subject I hope to enter more extensively elsewhere.

(2) One large part of the Exposition, namely De specialibus legibus, which is a great analysis of the Jewish Law to show how it is in practical harmony with the gentile jurisprudence of contemporary Egypt, seems to me wholly pointless as designed for Jews. But such an argument would be highly significant for gentiles like those described above, who had a great interest in the Jewish religion but retained the point of view toward legal administration set for them by the Roman prefect and *iuridicus*. Such gentiles would be impressed, much more than loyal Jews, by the fact that the Mosaic code could be practically harmonized with the Roman and Greek legal principles upon just those points that the iuridicus would have demanded from the Jews anyway.[12]

(3) The attitude of the Exposition to proselytes is significant. The Allegory mentions them virtually not at all, the Quaestiones very rarely, though at least one important passage there, to be quoted presently, does appear. But the Exposition not only makes frequent allusion to them and offers explanations adapted to them, but closes just before the final section on sanctions, with an eager exhortation to proselytes to come inside, and an elaborate explanation that εὐγένεια, the high birth of which the Jew was so proud, was not a matter of descent from Abraham, but of leaving, like Abraham, false teaching and sin for piety.[13] These passages are found in De virtutibus, which, as has been mentioned, Massebieau regarded as dependencies of De vita Mosis and as addressed to gentiles. They are no less obviously intended for gentiles now that it has been proved that they belong to the Exposition, with whose general and distinctive interest in gentiles and proselytes they are in complete accord.

(4) It is notable that in the Allegory Philo plainly indicates that for all his loyalty to the Torah its specific commands are often a heavy burden, while the truly pious will pass beyond the laws to the Law and Logos, or to God himself. Perhaps this attitude is implicit in the νόμοι ἔμψυχοι of the Exposition, but it would never be suspected from that document alone. Outspoken scorn for and rejection of the literal meaning of the Scriptures, such as appear in the Allegory,

---

[12]See my *Jewish Jurisprudence in Egypt.*

[13]The treatises De paenitentia and De nobilitate, in *De virtutibus* 175-227.

are totally lacking in the Exposition. Such an attitude toward the Holy Oracles, Philo seems to have felt, was too advanced for beginners and outsiders.[14]

(5) The Allegory assumes throughout that the reader, as a Jew, is so familiar with the Scriptures as to need only allusions, while the Exposition mentions nothing about the Scriptures or Judaism without explanation. It tells the stories of the Pentateuch with freedom and detail, apparently assuming that the reader has never heard them; it treats the religious customs of the Jews as quite unfamiliar to the reader and describes them. For example, it is hard to imagine a Jew in Alexandria of any level who would need to be told the following:

> But while [on the Sabbath] the Law forbids bodily labor, it requires the better types of activity, which are those carried on by words and teachings with respect to virtue. For it enjoins the spending of that time in philosophizing for the improvement of the soul and the dominant mind. So on the Sabbath there stand open throughout all cities ten thousand places of instruction in prudence, self-control, courage, justice, and the other virtues, in which the people sit quietly and in order, with ears alert and all attention by reason of their thirst for the refreshing words, while one of those more skilled stands and expounds the noblest, helpful principles by which the whole life shall advance to better things (De specialibus legibus ii. 61 f.).

The reader of this passage has apparently never even attended a synagogue service, and the fact that such an explanation was designed for a gentile becomes even more striking when it is recalled that the two other passages in Philo which describe the synagogue in almost exactly the same words are to be found in De vita Mosis ii. 215 f., and in the Apology (Hypothetica) as preserved in Eusebius, Praep. evang. viii. 7 (359d), both of which are admittedly addressed to gentiles.

A difficulty arises from the fact that what are now accepted as the concluding sections of De praemiis et poenis (§§ 79 ff.; in the edition of Cohn set off with the sub-titles, De benedictionibus and De exsecrationibus) are explicable only as designed for Jews. Jewish feeling on the part of the reader, his loyalty to the race, and his consequent love of the racial traditions and abhorrence of apostasy are everywhere assumed. If these must be kept as parts of the Exposition, the foregoing argument must be fallacious. But the fact is that their claim to be considered a part of De praemiis et poenis is at best tenuous, and seems to me to be essentially ill founded.

---

[14]Massebieau and Bréhier (note 10 above), pp. 182 ff., develop the contrast on this point between the Exposition and the Allegory. As they explain all other contrasts in Philo as coming from different periods of his life, so they do here, and as usual unconvincingly.

De praemiis et poenis, which was obviously intended as what Shürer calls an "epilogue" to the Exposition, begins with a survey of the entire preceding argument, and then discusses the rewards of the faithful, taking the rewards earned by the great patriarchs as a model. This section is completed, and Philo turns to the punishments. A passage is devoted to Clain, who was punished by being put into a state whereby he was always *in articulo mortis*, and then Philo begins with Korah and his company, whose punishment typified that visited upon households; but the book suddenly breaks off. The manuscripts go on, with no sign of a break, to what Cohn identified as another treatise, De benedictionibus, which itself ends with the statement that, having completed the matter of blessings, the author will go on to discuss curses. Here, according to the manuscripts, De praemiis et poenis is finished. A short treatise, quite separate in the manuscripts, is preserved with the title De exsecrationibus. This is indubitably the discussion to which Philo referred at the end of De benedictionibus, and so Cohn has correctly joined the two in his edition.[15] All of this material is thus put by Cohn under the title De praemiis et poenis, as a single treatise with three, or four, divisions, and his judgment has been accepted by Schürer[16] and Heinemann.[17] The possibility does not seem to have occurred to anyone that De benedictionibus, which thrusts itself so awkwardly into the text, may not belong to De praemiis et poenis at all, but may be another treatise put in with De praemiis et poenis by a copyist because the ending of that treatise had been lost or omitted, and this treatise, with a similar subject matter, was at hand to fill the gap. So far as the manuscript tradition goes, it is as justifiable to move De benedictionibus out of its setting and join it with De exsecrationibus as it is to move the latter over into De praemiis et poenis. And certainly one or the other has to be moved.

The external testimony to De benedictionibus is slight and ambiguous. It is quoted with a title twice by John of Damascus in the Sacra Parallela. The passage, p. 357, 5 ff. of Cohn's edition of De benedictionibus, appears in two manuscripts of the Sacra Parallela with the simple introduction Φίλωνος, but in a third manuscript at the same passage with the caption Φίλωνος ἐκ τοῦ περὶ ἄθλων καὶ ἐπιτιμίων; the passage, pp. 359, 18 to 360, 4, is quoted in three manuscripts of the Sacra Parallela, in one with the introduction Φίλωνος, in two with Φίλωνος ἐκ τοῦ περὶ εὐχῆς καὶ εὐλογιῶν. From these facts the only possible conclusion seems to be that in the manuscript used by John himself the two treatises, De praemiis et poenis and De benedictionibus, were united, but that the second treatise retained its original title, which has disappeared from our manuscripts of Philo but been restored by Cohn. De exsecrationibus is not quoted by any ancient writer. Eusebius does not quote any one of the three

---

[15]See the introduction to volume V, pp. xxviii f.

[16]Schürer, 4th ed., 1909, p. 675.

[17]In the publication begun under the editorship of L. Cohn and continued by Heinemann, *Die Werke Philos von Alexandria in deutscher Übersetzung,* II, 381.

treatises, but gives the title περὶ τῶν προκειμένων ἐν τῷ νόμῳ τοῖς μὲν ἀγαθοῖς ἄθλων, τοῖς δὲ πονηροῖς ἐπιτιμίων καὶ ἀρῶν..[18] Cohn argues, since he wants to include De exsecrationibus as part of De praemiis et poenis, that the title as Eusebius had it was really περὶ ἄθλων καὶ ἐπιτιμίων καὶ ἀρῶν. One's first response to this suggestion is that to make Eusebius refer to a work of three divisions, when his μὲν ... δέ so obviously implies a two-fold division, is a violation of Eusebius' Greek that needs considerable justification. I see no reason why Eusebius' form of the title should not be the one Philo himself gave to De praemiis et poenis apart from the other two treatises, for the doublet ἐπιτιμίων καὶ ἀρῶν is quite in accord with Philo's custom always to use two words when possible instead of one, and the text, when it turns to discuss penalties in the section still indubitably a part of De praemiis et poenis, actually is concerned with the curse (ἀρά) of Cain (§ 72). To see in Eusebius' title a reference to the treatise περὶ ἀρῶν is only justified by the scholar's desire to do so. So Eusebius' form of the title still leaves open the question of the inclusion of the two subtreatises as parts of De praemiis et poenis. As to these treatises, accordingly, we have only the witness of John of Damascus, which has led us to conclude that, in his manuscript of Philo, De benedictionibus was combined with De praemiis et poenis, but had a distinctive title. Since De praemiis et poenis is so obviously mutilated at § 78, just where De benedictionibus begins, the possibility seems to me open, so far as external testimony goes, that a process of absorption had begun at least by the time John's manuscript of Philo was composed, a process by which De benedictionibus had been taken into De praemiis et poenis, but which had not yet reached the stage represented by our manuscripts, where the original title of the absorbed treatise has disappeared.

The propriety of considering De benedictionibus and De exsecrationibus as parts of De praemiis et poenis is thus thrown entirely upon internal testimony.

De benedictionibus opens (§§ 79-84) with an appeal to the reader to obey the laws carefully, based upon the statement in Deut. 30, 10-14 that the Law should be in the Jew's mouth, heart, and hands. In discussing the passage Philo begins with the tenth verse, and makes the whole refer to the ἐντολαὶ καὶ προστάγματα. As a Jew to Jews he is promising in the messianic age deliverance from enemies, brute beasts as well as all hostile men. With this deliverance he promises authority over other peoples, wealth and prosperity so that the Jews will become the bankers of the world, and a sure line of succession so that no Jewish man or woman will be left without children. He who adheres to the holy laws will have a fulness of life, not only in quantity but quality (§§ 111-117), and will even be protected from disease (§§ 118 ff.). "These are the εὐχαί for good men, who fulfill the laws in their actions," Philo concludes (§

---

[18]Eusebius, H. E. ii, 18, 5.

126). Repentance is mentioned, but it is the repentance of the erring Jew who is called back to the true life from having been led astray by pleasure.

> As God can easily by a single command gather together men who are scattered in the ends of the earth, bringing them back from the uttermost limits to whatever single place he may choose,

so he can bring back the lost soul into the true path (§ 117).

De exsecrationibus goes on with the reverse side of the picture in exactly the same way. Long and vivid sections are devoted to the poverty and ruin (§§ 127-136), the enslavement to gentiles (§§ 137-142), the bodily diseases of all kinds (§§ 143-147), the complete loss of spirit (§§ 148, 151), the exposure to wild beasts (§ 149), which God will bring upon Jews who do not keep his laws (§§ 138, 142). The upright proselyte (immigrant, ἔπηλυς) will be a shame to the Jews who have corrupted the coinage of their εὐγένεια (§ 152) and must watch these outsiders taking the rewards designed for themselves. All the Jew's feeling of superiority is manifest in this reference to proselytes. Philo specifies some of the laws the breaking of which will bring such destruction. They are first the failure to observe the sabbatical year of the fields and the sabbath, violation of the salt and truce, [19] and of the altar of mercy and the common hearth.[20] The great emphasis laid upon the sabbatical rest for the soil suggests that Philo had farmers especially in mind as his audience. The virtues are briefly mentioned as the ideal (§ 160), but Philo then turns again to the laws the violation of which is to be followed by horrible catastrophe, and this time he inveighs especially (§ 162) against leaving the laws altogether to adopt polytheistic opinions (πολύθεοι δόξαι). A call to repentance is given, which is again a return of the wanderer to the fold and will be followed by the gathering together of the scattered and enslaved Jews. Their virtues will make their masters flee from them in fear (§§ 164 ff.). In this will be made manifest the mercy of God, the power of the founders of the nation as intercessors with God for their descendants, and the trueness of their repentance by which they now please God as sons do a father (§§ 166 f.). Then the dignity and prosperity of the race will be restored and vindicated before all men.

The strong messianic fervor of these treatises, their intense Jewish patriotism, and above all the emphasis upon the importance for good or ill of the specific and literal laws, are unique in Philo's writings. Yet this is so much in

---

[19]These refer to the obligations of hospitality, joined in that connection in De specialibis legibus iii. 96.

[20]The altar of mercy and common hearth can only refer to the household hearth of refuge which Alexandrine Jews seem to have brought into Judaism from Greek custom. See Heinemann's note ad loc. in *Die Werke Philos von Alexandria in deutscher Übersetzung,* and my *Jurisprudence of the Jewish Courts in Egypt,* pp. 53 ff.; also Heinemann, *Philons grieschische und jüdische Bildung,* pp. 344 f.

accord with the type of Jewish pride and loyalty which Philo manifests toward the race and the laws in In Flaccum and Legatio ad Gaium that there is no reason to doubt that it is the sort of popular address Philo would have made to an assembly of his countrymen.

That such a peroration could have concluded the Exposition is another matter. The μετάνοια he is urging in the Exposition is not that of the wanderer returning to the fold, but that of one who, having been brought up in heathenism, changes over to become a servant of God. If men will repent in this sense, God promises them citizenship in the noblest πολιτεία (De virtutibus 175). The repentance he here visualizes is that of the immigrants (ἐπηλύται, § 182), whose chief business in repenting is to forsake the training which their early teachers gave them (§ 178). They are contrasted with apostates, who abandon their holy laws (§ 182), but when Philo explains these holy laws, he turns to the same passage in Deut. 30 with an entirely different interpretation from that in De benedictionibus. For in De virtutibus he omits verse 10 with its reference to ἐντολαί, and makes the invitation in the passage not to loyalty to the specific and individual commands, but to a life of virtue such as the true worship of God found in Judaism inculcates. De praemiis et poenis is animated by exactly the same spirit. The Judaism that is finally being approved in the great sanctions of rewards and punishments has not the slightest reference to obedience to detailed commands, but is the Judaism which looks primarily to the patriarchs; by imitating their characters and their attitude toward God, and by sharing their spirit, men may hope for the same rewards as they. The patriarchs appeared in De exsecrationibus, but as heavenly intercessors, not as models and present working influences in men's lives. The specific laws are not repudiated in any part of the Exposition; on the contrary Philo goes to great lengths, too great lengths as Heinemann rightly thinks,[21] in defending them. But having defended them he can now safely ignore them, so as to conclude with what he has had in mind throughout, a philosophic and mystical Judaism in which they have no essential place. From this elaborately developed structure, it is unthinkable that Philo, after any conceivable sort of transitional paragraphs, could have turned to such an address to Jews as De benedictionibus and De exsecrationibus.

My own guess is that the Christian copyists who have preserved our manuscript tradition of Philo from long before the time of John of Damascus, found the ending of De praemiis et poenis too strong an invitation to Judaism to keep. They dropped it out, and concealed the omission (or filled out a folio) by putting De benedictionibus in its place, at first preserving the original title of that treatise, but later omitting even this. But by whatever chance the change occurred, De benedictionibus and De exsecrationibus cannot have been parts of the Exposition.

---

[21]*Philons griechische und jüdische Bildung*, pp. 572-574.

The Exposition is thus more intelligible throughout when, in contrast with the writings designed for Jews, it is recognized to have been written for gentiles. In that case the last objection disappears to the thesis that the Exposition and De vita Mosis were companion pieces. They are similar in literary character and in that respect present the same contrasts to the writings designed for Jews. De vita Mosis forecasts the argument of the Exposition, and the Exposition includes De vita Mosis in its summary of the points covered.

De vita Mosis was written, it is my conclusion, to serve as the first presentation of the Jewish point of view to be given to a gentile who showed genuine interest in the Jews but as yet knew little about them. To a gentile less open minded would probably have been offered the Hypothetica in order to disabuse his mind of prejudices instilled by opponents of the Jews. However that may be, De vita Mosis was ready for those interested and sympathetic. If the treatise succeeded in its purpose, it would awaken an interest in the reader to go on to the more detailed exposition of the Pentateuch suggested in De vita Mosis itself. To meet this latter, more advanced, gentile demand Philo wrote the Exposition. This explained first the relation of God to the world and to the Mosaic Code, and then passed on to the great νόμοι ἔμψυχοι who were the real saviours of Judaism; then, omitting the life of Moses as already covered, it proceeded to the decalogue, in which the principles of the laws of nature were expressed, and next to the specific laws, as highly workable practicable statutes not only in harmony with natural law and the decalogue, but entirely observable under Greek and Roman administration. The ritual law, on the other hand, was shown to represent the ideal mystery-religion, of cosmic rather than national significance. The argument was concluded by a demonstration of the place of some of the great Hellenistic virtues in the system, an exhortation to gentiles to be converted, and a review of the entire argument, including De vita Mosis, closing with a statement of the sanctions of the Jewish system, as here interpreted, in divine rewards and punishments.

De vita Mosis and the Exposition together are a body of evidence for the character of Jewish propaganda among gentiles of much greater importance than has been appreciated. A careful analysis of them from that point of view would teach us much about the actual religious position of "God-fearers" and proselytes[22] in the Hellenistic-Roman World.

---

[22]Philo does not himself make this familiar distinction. His "proselytes" need not be circumcised: see *Quaestiones in Exodum* ii. 2; R. Harris, *Fragments of Philo Judaeus*, p. 49.

Chapter Six

Wolfson's *Philo*

Journal of Biblical Literature 1948, 67:87-109

Few scholars these days try to produce anything which could be called a *magnum opus*. Wolfson is one of the few; and when it is remembered that the two large volumes before us[1] represent a relatively small part of his total undertaking, he must be put into the forefront of even that little group. For it is Wolfson's plan to present a history of philosophy which will begin with at least one volume on the Greeks, then consider Philo as here, then give the whole development of philosophy in Christian, Islamic, and Jewish circles of the Middle Ages, and finally show the beginnings of the new age where Spinoza breaks the pattern of medieval thought and returns to the Greek approach. Wolfson believes that medieval philosophy had a distinctive character because it had a distinctive source of knowledge quite foreign to both the Greek and modern thinkers, the source we usually call "revelation," but which Wolfson calls the "preamble of faith" (p. v). The moderns, like the Greeks, try by observation, hypothesis, and intuition, whatever these words mean, to discover the truth about the nature of man, and the nature of his environment up to and including God himself. The medieval world had to square all such data of "reason" with the data of their inspired Scriptures where the answers were all given. More than this, the medievalists had to square their reasons with a philosophical tradition which determined how Scripture itself was to be interpreted, Wolfson says, for in religion they had "a set of inflexible principles of a divinely revealed origin, by which philosophy, the product of erring human reason, had to be tested and purged and purified." These inflexible principles, Wolfson continues in his Preface, were all worked out by none other than Philo himself, and so "the philosophy of Philo" came to be "the most dominant force in the history of philosophy down to the seventeenth century."

Even as ardent a Philonist as myself must blink at so great a claim for our hero. That the Philonic school, or hellenized Judaism, was one of the most important formative influences in the making of Christianity; that it set a

---

[1] Harry Austryn Wolfson, *Philo: Foundations of Religious Philosophy in Judaism, Christianity, and Islam* (Structure and Growth of Philosophic Systems from Plato to Spinoza, II). Cambridge, Massachusetts: Harvard University Press, 1947. Pp. I, xvi + 462; II, 531.

tendency and method whose elaboration does distinguish medieval thought from the thinking of ancient and modern times; that this was largely a requirement to hold reason within the limits of revealed religion – these seem to me clearly indisputable, though medieval thinkers steadily forced so much into the words of Scripture that the "limits of revealed religion" became highly debatable entities. Wolfson, however, wants to go farther and to see in a single "set of inflexible principles," a single "philosophy," that of Philo, the dominating force in all later medieval thinking. Wolfson's volumes on Philo attempt to show how this "philosophy," these "inflexible principles," came into existence in the mind of one who was, Wolfson says (I, 114) "a philosopher in the grand manner."

The volumes on Philo are so impressive as they stand on the shelves, and as one reads their amazingly detailed exposition, that already it is being said on many sides that the "definitive" work on Philo has at last appeared. Since Philo is (or should be) carefully studied by NT scholars as well as by historians of Judaism, it is well to give the work a closer scrutiny than is allowed in any ordinary review.

Wolfson approaches his task with what seems to be an inexhaustible knowledge of the writings of all ancient and medieval writers. Out of this universe he has come to abstract elements common to all these writers which he is right in seeing brought together for the first time in Philo's writings. Wolfson takes this preconceived distillation of medieval philosophers, and finding most of it in Philo he calls it "Philo" himself. Philo is to him the dramatic point where revelation entered to dominate reason. And the revelation which came into Western thought through Philo seems for Wolfson to be specifically Jewish revelation. What Wolfson is really demonstrating is that medieval thought began with the confluence of Greek and Jewish points of view. In this large issue Philo the person is quite secondary.

For, to go back a step farther, in Philo there joined with Greek rationalism (as Wolfson considers the Greek stream to be) a Judaism which Wolfson seems to have learned not from Philo at all but from rabbinical tradition which he interprets much as George Foote Moore did. Moore's "normative" Judaism seems to have become Wolfson's less fortunate "native" Judaism,[2] but it is still the same condensation of halachic rabbinism as that which Moore represented as a norm in the thinking of all Jews from the time of Ezra, or shortly afterwards, to the present. This tradition included, or course, the notion that all human thought and conduct must be regulated by the divinely inspired Torah. It included much more; and Wolfson will have us believe that the Judaism of Philo is, in amazing detail, the Judaism of "native Jewish tradition." So in two introductory chapters Wolfson describes the formation of the Diaspora; how Jews went out with their Bibles, and "native Jewish tradition," and were attracted by the systematic reasoning of classical Greek philosophers (especially Plato and Aristotle), but imposed upon that reasoning the theistic points of view of revealed Judaism, the halachic respect for law as statute, the hatred of polytheism and idolatry, and Jewish eschatology. In such an approach to Philo one sees steadily at work the mind of a person who recognizes kinship between Philo and that tradition at places where an ordinary reader would (and could) never do. Consequently, these details take on an engrossing importance for Wolfson; they make him stress "native" details out of proportion to their place in Philo's thinking, and blind him to the very existence of much in Philo which has a character quite foreign to "native Judaism."

As a consequence Wolfson at no place prepares the reader to find in Philo a writer who reads as a whole so utterly unlike either Plato or the rabbis. Granted that Philo is writing Jewish midrash, his *Allegories,* or the writings in his *Exposition,* are startlingly unlike the Tannaitic Midrashim of which Wolfson makes so much use. Wolfson sees in Philo so many details which resemble details of rabbinic tradition, and so completely ignores the Jewish details which are unlike it, that he misses entirely the dissimilar totality. From the Greek side Philo's writings are just as little to be described as Plato and Aristotle imposed upon Jewish midrash. For from this side too the presence of strikingly Platonic

---

[2]"Native Jewish Tradition" as a word for halachic (with a little haggadic) rabbinical tradition seems to me even more unfortunate than Moore's "normative," because at least the word "normative" meant something. I suspect Wolfson himself would deny either meaning I have been able to construe for the term "native," but confess I cannot guess what meaning he would give it. For I can see only two possible meanings: 1) That it is the religion of those who are "native Jews" in the sense of having been born of Jewish parents. But the extreme variety of native Jewish belief in this sense robs the term of any specific meaning. Philo was as well born a native Jew as Akiba. 2) That it is a tradition natively produced within Judaism, and with no accretions from the outside. But such a Judaism never existed. Canaanite influence, Syrian influence, Babylonian influence, Persian influence (I dare not mention Greek influence), all these came in to color even the strictest rabbinic thought. If the "tradition" has many non-Jewish ancestors, and many Jews did not hold the tradition, it is perplexing to know in what sense it is "native." As Wolfson uses it, it means Moore's normative Judaism, or rabbinic Judaism, made to include, if not be, a touch here and there from apocryphal, gnomic, and apocalyptic literatures.

and Aristotelian elements and individual ideas blinds Wolfson to what has been recently more and more apparent, that the whole Greek manner of thinking in Philo, certainly has manner of presenting non-Jewish ideas, is as foreign to the rationalism of Plato and Aristotle as it is to the manner or matter of the Tannaitic Midrashim.

That is, anyone trained in Plato and Aristotle, and familiar with rabbinic literature, but who had not read Philo, could not but be completely convinced by Wolfson's study. For here detailed similarities between quotations from Philo and quotations from these Greek and Jewish sources accumulate almost infinitely, and conviction comes with the accumulation. If, however, the same reader then turned to Philo himself, and from Philo to such writings on Philo as those of Conybeare, Pascher, and others, he would be puzzled indeed to find a Philo, completely documented and dominant, to whose thinking Wolfson alludes only in his introductory chapters where he hurriedly denies his existence. Wolfson tells us at the beginning (I, 36-55) that he finds no mysticism, no kinship to the mystery religions, in Philo: I suspect that he does so because except in these few pages of special pleading Wolfson ignores all Philo's mysticism and mystical conceptions.

On this section we must stop a moment. Wolfson begins by pointing out what has commonly been recognized by all students of Philo, that Philo abhorred and denounced Greek worship, mysteries, and mythologies, in spite of the fact that he often used the vocabulary of the mysteries, and made literary allusions to the myths. No one has ever suggested, to my knowledge, that Philo accepted Greek or Egyptian mythology or cultus as such. The real issue is the vocabulary of the mysteries: did Philo use it "as he uses terms borrowed from popular religion and from mythology, all of them because they were part of common speech" (I, 46), as Wolfson thinks, that is stripped of any literal meaning; or did he "identify, by means of allegory, the religion of Scripture with the religion of the mysteries," so that "thereby 'Judaism was at once transformed into the greatest, the only true, Mystery'" (I, 45, quoting from my *By Light, Light,* 7)?

It must at once be admitted that Philo would agree with Wolfson in repudiating such a statement as representing what he was trying to do. "Identify the religion of Scripture with the religion of the mysteries" would have been fighting words to Philo. For in this Wolfson shows how completely he misses the point of all who see a real similarity between Philo's religious thinking and that of such people as Plutarch and Apuleius and the later Neo-Platonists like Proclus. Mystic Judaism was not, to Philo, just another mystery religion, to be "identified" with the others. Rather it was, to Philo, in sharpest contrast to them. Philo did "identify" (Wolfson's term, not mine) the two in that he took the concepts of the mysteries over as living forces and ideals into his Judaism, but he did so quite unconsciously, and would indignantly have denied that he did so. "The more they borrowed, the more they must seem to themselves to repudiate" is a statement I have used elsewhere as the key to the fact that such people as Philo both borrow and repudiate. Because Philo would undoubtedly have denied with anger any suggestion that he borrowed anything from hellenistic and mystic religiosity to put into Jewish tradition, Wolfson denies it for him. But in doing so he denies, as Philo would have done, much that is obviously a part of Philo just the same.

So Wolfson devotes the next ten pages to discussing, or to paraphrasing, the passages where Philo speaks of Jewish religion in most directly mystic terms. If the mystic Israelites are guided to tame the passions by "some divine inspiration," that inspiration, Wolfson says, is "the laws of Moses," and the "practice of virtue" is itself "practice of the laws of Moses." The mystic intercourse by which God "sows and begets happiness in human souls," as Philo calls it, is to Wolfson the freedom which comes from God to one who is guided by the Law of Moses. The direct vision of God which Philo wanted to get "apart from God's Powers," and "not from created things" is knowledge of God got by revelation, that is, Wolfson explains by cross reference (II, 90) by "a direct perception of the evidence in nature for the existence of God which one may acquire with the help of God my means of prophecy and revelation." Accordingly, Wolfson asserts, men initiated into mysteries in Judaism meant to Philo "men of good native abilities and proper education who have succeeded in mastering their passions and in acquiring a true knowledge of the existence and nature of God" (I, 49). The mystic marriage, Wolfson goes on, is properly the "unbroken and constant union between God and man, for God is in a sense always in men" (I, 51). On this basis Philo rejects the heathen mysteries as mummeries, for "This is the meaning of Philo's comparison of the covenant between Israel and God to initiation into mysteries" *(ibidem)*. When Philo demands that the Jewish mystery, its "secret cakes" and the rest, be kept secret Wolfson interprets this as a cautioning against teaching the methods of allegory to uneducated and immoral men. Similar cautioning, Wolfson says, is to be found in the teaching of the rabbis, who warned against teaching widely the secret doctrines of the Chariot and of Creation (I, 55).

The implication of this final comparison is that the Mysteries of the Chariot and of Creation were similar to Philonic teaching, an idea with which one may in large part agree, at least as a real possibility. But the further implication that these Mysteries were an esoteric and revered part of rabbinic Judaism itself is something quite unjustified. Of these teachings we know almost nothing except that the rabbis wanted them not only kept from popular ears, but threatened damnation even to any rabbi who would listen to them. To refer to these Mysteries as rabbinic parallels to Philo's mystic Judaism is then, to say the least, strange. To say that Philo's warnings "mean nothing more than that rule laid down by the rabbis" cannot stand for a moment. Philo was as anxious to have his mystic Judaism taught to those competent to hear them as were the rabbis to suppress the other Mysteries altogether.

   This is Wolfson's total exposition of the mystic elements in Philo's
writings. For Philo as for hellenistic Jews in general the use of terms from
mystic philosophy, like the use of terms from Greek religious practices "was a
Hellenization in language only, not in belief or cult ... It did not cause them to
change their conception of their own religion" (I, 13). The subject is finally
dismissed without examining a single passage in its context. So throughout the
two volumes he need not refer once to the "Light-Stream," never discuss the
Patriarchs or their wives for their place in Philo's thinking, no once use the term
νόμος ἔμψυχος, or allude to the mystic celebration of the festivals. To the
mystic pattern as exemplified in the migrations of Abraham and of Jacob and of
Israel from Egypt Wolfson never refers, or to the miraculous babies, Isaac and
Moses. Hence for all that is impressive in Wolfson's massive alignment of
fragments of Philo with parallel fragments from Plato, Aristotle, and the rabbis,
he has never once tried to get into step with the marching of Philo's own mind
as revealed in his writings. With not the least regard for the process and sweep
of Philo's own exposition, Wolfson shatters it into bits and presents us with a
"Philo" by picking up what fragments he can put into a mosaic of his own
design.

   To Wolfson Philo must be made a systematic philosopher who produced, by
uniting rabbinic Judaism with Plato and Aristotle, the dominant philosophy of
the Middle Ages. So Wolfson can never leave Philo in inconsistencies on any
point. "Unless we assume that Philo did not know his own mind, or that he
changed his mind, a way must be found to reconcile this statement with his
other statements" (I, 275). "By this interpretation of Philo we have been able to
remove all apparent inconsistencies" (I, 375). "There are no inconsistencies in
Philo on this point; there are only incomplete statements which have to be
completed by a comparison with other statements" (I, 382). The one conclusion
about Philo on which scholars had all agreed was that Philo frequently did not
"know his own mind," and just as frequently "changed" it. Wolfson's ingenuity
in combining isolated passages, in "completing" statements so as to reconcile
inconsistencies, brings inevitably to mind the word *pilpul*, an honored term in
rabbinic circles for this sort of analysis. Philo himself, in reconciling
statements of Scripture with each other and with Greek philosophy and
mysticism, or with common sense, was one of Wolfson's few superiors in the
art. Isolated instances of Wolfson's ingenuity such as appear in connection with
the sentences just quoted from his book might here be given, and will appear in
other connections, but a few instances cannot give the almost hypnotic force of a
thousand pages of such artistry. If one reads the writings of Philo long enough
one begins to wonder whether some of the mystic or philosophic notions he
finds in the Torah may not have been actually in the minds of the original
writers of the passages. One must be elaborately forewarned, and know the dates
of much that Wolfson quotes, not to feel that Wolfson similarly is making his
case.

For, with all mystic possibilities *a priori* dismissed from Philo, Wolfson can go on to show how Philo combined rabbinic Judaism with classical Greek rationalism. To do this Wolfson creates a most interesting background for Philo in both Judaism and Greek philosophy.

Actually Philo now appears to us as an island in the sea of antiquity, an island which must originally have been connected with the Greek mainland on one side, and the Jewish continent on the other. But this direct connection has been submerged by the loss of documents from his contemporaries and predecessors in both Hellenism and Judaism. In trying to reconstruct these lost connections between Philo and his environments Wolfson has two distinct methods, one of which he uses for the Greek relations of Philo, the other for the Jewish.

On the Greek side Philo has seemed to all his recent students who know Hellenistic philosophy in its mystic, Neo-Platonic, and Neo-Pythagorean developments to belong essentially with those schools. True we know these schools almost entirely from writers who lived after Philo. We have not a single document from a Platonist or Aristotelian after Aristotle (except Philo himself) until we get to the little *Introduction* of Albinus, over a century after Philo, and then to the great new world of Plotinus. All other schools of philosophy before Philo are similarly represented only by fragments, except for the little pseudo-Aristotelian *De Mundo*. Tradition which has gathered about the name of Plotinus' teacher puts the beginning of Neo-Platonism well back into the second century, but that is at least a century after the death of Philo. Cicero shows us some aspects of hellenistic thinking before Philo, and Seneca and Plutarch just after Philo. True, Plutarch approaches religious problems in a way to remind us often of Philo, but Philo obviously could not have read Plutarch, who was born about the year Philo must have died. After Plotinus comes the bewildering age of Porphyry, Julian, Proclus, Symmachus, Iamblichus, and the rest who in discussing popular religion go beyond Plutarch, but again only develop in greater elaboration much the sort of attitude which Plutarch himself showed. What then may we conclude that the Platonists of Alexandria in Philo's day taught? Did they read Plato and Aristotle in antiquarian devotion, or had they already begun to stress the mystical aspects of Plato, and see the possibility of their symbolic representation in current mystery religions as Philo himself seems to most of his students to read Plato into his Jewish Scriptures, if not into his Jewish cultus, and as Plutarch certainly did a few years later with pagan myth and cult?

These are questions we cannot answer with certainty, since we have no documents from philosophers who might have been Philo's personal teachers. It has, however, been generally supposed that with Philo showing so much that was akin to later theories of emanation and of mystic identification and ascent, the mystic development of Platonism and Stoicism had already begun before Philo, and that it was this new type of philosophy, shot full to be sure with the phraseology of the older teachers, but essentially oriented not in critical but in mystic thinking, which Philo had from his environment, and was trying to find expressed in his Judaism.

For Wolfson the problem does not exist. Since every document of importance which shows mystic philosophy comes from a writer like Plutarch who lived a half century after Philo, or from the chief Neo-Platonists and Gnostics who lived several centuries later, they are all irrelevant and can be completely ignored in discussing Philo's philosophical background. Neo-Platonism does not appear as an entry at all in Wolfson's elaborate Index. The *Hermetica* are mentioned in only a single passage (II, 114), along with the pseudo-Aristotelian *De Mundo,* Dio Chrysostom, Seneca, Maximus of Tyre, and Celsus. Geffcken and Norden had quoted these to show that there was a Greek tradition that God is nameless, and that when Philo talked of the namelessness of God he was drawing upon the tradition to which these writers attest. None of them is relevant to the discussion, Wolfson asserts, because "with the exception of Seneca, who was a contemporary of Philo, all these sources are later than Philo." With these thus dismissed, Wolfson goes on to derive Philo's notion that God is not named from Jewish sources, a section which he summarizes: "In Scripture Philo has found (a) statements to the effect that God has not revealed His name to those to whom He appeared and also (b) laws prohibiting (1) to mention the proper name of God, (2) to take in vain any other name of God and (3) to treat lightly the word 'God' in general. Scripture thus teaches the doctrine of the unnamability of God" (II, 126). By this time Wolfson has quite lost sight of land. Nothing is clearer in the Torah and Talmud alike than that God has a name, "Yahweh," and that it must not be pronounced because the name itself has so much power. The notion of the namelessness of God is essentially foreign to Judaism, and none of the proof-texts Wolfson discusses to make the notion scriptural would ever have suggested such an idea to Philo or anyone else *de novo.* But Wolfson will not allow it to be Greek. In spite of the fact that the idea is so essentially foreign to Judaism, and the plain meaning of many Greek writers, it is not Greek, for "No philosopher, as we have seen, ever said so explicitly" (II, 119).

Wolfson lists (I, 93 f.) the Greek philosophers from Philo quotes, the only ones, we see as we go on, who can legitimately be examined as possible sources for Philo's thinking. The mystical philosophers are by this method all excluded, since those whose names we know are all later than Philo, and they need not be mentioned. Philo was drawing only upon the earlier critical philosophers.

One can defend such a method of study, perhaps, up to a point. Philo is to be explained only out of what fragments we have of his known predecessors, a method which works very well if only those statements in Philo are examined which can be shown to resemble statements found in those known predecessors (or else are Jewish in origin). If this limitation of Philo's sources to his known predecessors were followed out logically, and all of Philo taken into consideration, one would have to conclude that Philo was the inventor of Gnostic and Neo-Platonic thought-ways, since in embryo these ways are so much his own, and since such thought-ways come to us for the first time in Philo's writings. That conclusion would be an argument from silence which few would care to advance, but it could be advanced just the same. Wolfson does not reach that conclusion only because he resolutely omits every mystical elements, phrase, or passage which he possibly can, and explains away, as in the case of the namelessness of God, what of it he feels forced to include.

If this method were to be accepted to determine Philo's debt to the gentiles, it would have, however, to apply also to the Jewish sources, in which no document (or at least no rabbinical saying) could ever be quoted for "native Jewish tradition" which could not confidently be dated before Philo. For Philo's Jewish background presents much the same problem as the Greek. The rabbinic sayings and documents which we can date actually before Philo are extremely scattered and inadequate, and we can reconstruct his Jewish milieu from extra-Philonic sources with no greater confidence than his Greek.

In the first place we shall never agree about the religious life of Palestine itself. What relation had the Sadducean to the Pharisaic points of view in Philo's day? How far at that time had rabbinic tradition developed toward the formation of the Mishna and the Midrash? How great influence did either Pharisees or Sadducees have in the religious life of the mass of Jews in Palestine, and if they had influence in what sort of paths would they have been leading? Where do the apocalyptic writings fit in, and how much interest in Messianism, and in what sort of Messianism, had the mass of Jews then? Still more problematic is the origin of Jewish life and worship as these appear in rabbinic tradition itself: where did Jews learn to use a blessed cup of wine in marriage, in the Seder, in circumcision, and at the beginning and ending of every Sabbath and festival, and what did it originally mean that it should still, like Greek usage, be so intimately connected with fire, light, life, and immortality? What did the mass of Jews even in Palestine really think of the religious observances of their gentile neighbors that they took in so many of the gentile customs? Of course we have such protests as those of the books of Maccabees: but these books themselves seem to tell of popular (and largely permanent) departures from the strict laws of the "pious ones" of that period quite as much as they tell of the political victories of the pious. I had almost said "of the pious minorities," but this matter of majority and minority also we do not know.

Not one of these questions can be answered with any demonstration or finality. That Wolfson or I have theories about all of this, that Graetz, Moore, Baron, Marx, Schürer, Finkelstein, Bousset, and a host of others, have or had theories, only shows that for the religious situation in Palestine at the time of Philo we have nothing but theories, not answers with which we can, by adequate evidence, force all fair minds to agree. In the absence of an established norm or a total picture, *the religious point of view of the author of each document which survives from the period must be reconstructed out of that document itself,* and its relation to any other document or tradition is the end, not the beginning, of our search. George Foote Moore's "normative Judaism," for example, was a reconstruction of a religious totality out of a few rabbinic fragments ascribed to the period before the destruction of the temple, along with a host of other fragments from a later period. It was a norm which he devised and applied for his own convenience, but never showed at all to be a generally recognized norm by all Jews of the period, though he projected his construct back into the Judaism of the first century, and thought it actually existed there. So he brushed apocalyptic Judaism out into the lunatic fringe, and regarded Philo as a person, like Melchizedek, without ancestors or descendants, a unique phenomenon, curious but quite unimportant for any picture of Judaism itself. It is not to be questioned that rabbinic Judaism, Moore's "normative" Judaism, had laid firm foundations by Philo's time, or that as it later developed this Judaism from the sixth century after Christ to the present was recognized generally as "orthodox" or "normative" (though many Cabbalists and Chassidim might question it). What we do now know is whether "normative Judaism" was normative even in Palestine for the mass of Jews before Philo's time.

Still less to be reconstructed from non-Philonic writings is the Judaism of the Diaspora, specifically of Alexandria. We must grant without reservation Wolfson's contention that the Jews who came to Alexandria with their revered Torah brought also a tradition (or, as he does not suggest, various traditions) of its interpretation. In regarding Jerusalem as the center of their piety and in going there as often as possible for their festivals, Jews must have learned much from procedures in Jerusalem. But what all this added up to as a background for Philo and influence in his thinking we have only the writings of Philo himself to tell us. The scraps from pre-Philonic writers quoted by Eusebius, the scattered books like Aristeas and 2-4 Maccabees, are of great value, but present no coherent picture which we can take as a norm to apply to Philo, or to Alexandrian Judaism in general.

Moore was sufficiently realistic to recognize that Philo did not fit into his "normative" picture. Wolfson would have us believe that Moore's "normative" Judaism, or as he calls it "native Jewish tradition" not only existed in Philo's day, but existed clearly in Philo's mind as the norm for his Judaism. Wolfson's method of demonstrating this is on scores of points to quote "native Jewish tradition" in parallel with statements of Philo. But here, in contrast with his rigid exclusion of all Greek sources not specifically earlier than Philo, Wolfson is amazingly uncritical. To be sure, in trying to show that Philo depended upon "native Jewish tradition" on any given point Wolfson does cite as a parallel the earliest appearance of the notion in a rabbinic source, but in few instances can he cite a parallel from a rabbi earlier than Philo, and most of his citations must be dated very much after him.

Philo's interpretation of one passage of the Bible, says Wolfson (II, 226 f.), "is already found in native Jewish literature." The impression from Wolfson's way of writing is that "already" means that the idea is found in literature antecedent to Philo; but the "literature" Wolfson cites is the *Mekilta of Rabbi Simeon ben Yohai*, a tannaitic writing of the School of Akiba, whose author flourished nearly a century after Philo had died, fifty years later than Plutarch. This material Wolfson amplifies by quotations from Rashi of the eleventh century, the *Sefer Miswot Gadol*, completed in 1250, and the *'Ammude Golah*, likewise of the thirteenth century.[3] Now it is freely to be admitted that these writings, even the medieval ones, contain much early material, much of which must even antedate Philo; but the passage in the *Mekilta* to which Wolfson refers, according to Rabbi Sandmel who kindly looked it up for me, is referred to no rabbi by name at all, and so must be presumed to be a second century interpretation. Such a use of Jewish sources to reconstruct the Jewish background of Philo, use which takes from these later writings any convenient passage at random to assert that it is material "already found in native Jewish literature," is indeed loose and misleading.

The trouble is that this is not an isolated instance, a lapse such as every one makes, but the sort of demonstration of which his two volumes largely consist.

In I, 247 Wolfson says: "By the time of Philo the term 'place' as an appellation of God was already in common Jewish usage in Palestinian Judaism." But his earliest evidence for this is a statement from Rabbi Jose ben Halafta of the late second century after Christ. I have no objection to the notion that this is a term which came to Philo from a very old Jewish tradition reaching back into Palestine itself, though there is no evidence to show it. Certainly Wolfson goes completely beyond his evidence when he says that by Philo's time the term was "in common Jewish usage in Palestine."

At II, 222 f. Wolfson points out that Philo represents the command to honor one's parents as being "'on the border-line between the human and the divine' [quoting from Philo], for 'parents are to their children what God is to the world.' In native Jewish tradition the same view is expressed in the statement that 'Scripture places the honoring of father and mother on a level with the honoring of God.'" This last Wolfson quotes from the *Mekilta of Ishmael*[4] with other parallels, at the earliest a century and a half after Philo was writing. The implication however is that in these we have documented the original of Philo's idea. To establish such a relationship not only does Wolfson by implication misrepresent the actual date of the "native" tradition, but by inadequately quoting Philo on the point he misrepresents Philo's own thinking, which was here

---

[3]These dates and the following are taken from H. L. Strack, *Introduction to the Talmud and Midrash* (1931), or the *Jewish Encyclopedia*.

[4]Most conveniently consulted in the edition and translation by J. Z. Lauterbach (1933), II, 257 f., where this saying is referred to "Rabbi," who was born in 135 A.D.

purely Greek. For Philo says that parents are θεοὶ ἐμφανεῖς, "manifest gods," who in begetting their children become creators parallel to God the creator.[5] That is the reason they "are to their children what God is to the world." That parents might in any sense be called "gods" would have scandalized the rabbis, so Wolfson finds it convenient not to mention that Philo says so. But there is no reason to suppose any relation whatever between Philo's notion of parents and the late and quite different statements Wolfson quotes from the rabbis.

Again, Philo discusses why Moses should have begun the Torah, a book of laws, with the story of Creation, and shows that this story is a proëmium, as the Greeks called it, an introduction of a kind which has suggested to many of Philo's students the Pythagorean proëmia to codes of laws, a few of which have survived.[6] Ignoring this, Wolfson quotes (II, 209 f.) from the *Tanhuma* to show that in the passage Philo is following "native Jewish tradition." The *Tanhuma* is a collection of material begun in the fifth century after Christ, and finally completed much later, a typical mixture of a little quite early material (almost nothing from before the second century after Christ) with a great deal centuries later in origin. From this, without discussing the date of the particular material, Wolfson quotes from "a rabbi" that "the story of creation as well as the subsequent historical part [of the Torah] is for the purpose of 'making known the power of His might'." "Philo similarly says," Wolfson continues, that the story of creation demonstrates that "since God is the creator of the world and the founder of the laws of nature, the Law for human guidance which was subsequently revealed by him is in harmony with these laws of nature." Wolfson goes on to report Philo as thinking that Moses designed the historical part of the Torah to demonstrate the existence and providence of God.

In this rabbinic "parallel" not only is the "rabbi's" date so uncertain as to make his evidence quite dubious for Philo's background, but the ideas expressed by Philo and the "rabbi" are quite different. Any apparent similarity evaporates when we see what Philo actually said in the passage. Philo says that he who would "use the laws [of Moses] must be a happy follower of nature and live according to the ordering of the universe" (τοῦ ὅλου);[7] "harmony with the universe" (τοῦ παντός), Philo shortly says,[8] is "agreement with the Logos of Nature." In reporting these statements Wolfson has reversed the singular and plural. While Philo talks of the Jewish laws (plural) as in harmony with Nature (singular), and says that agreement with the order (singular) of the universe is agreement with the Logos (singular) of Nature, Wolfson makes obedience to the Jewish Law (singular) a conformity to the laws (plural) of nature. The shift is

---

[5]See my *The Jurisprudence of the Jewish Courts in Egypt*, 67 ff.

[6]See É. Bréhier, *Les idées philosophiques et religieus de Philon d'Alexandrie* (1908 or 1925), p. 24. Colson thinks the allusion is to Plato's *Laws* and *Republic*, perhaps also to Zeno; see his translation VI, 472, n.

[7]*Mos.* ii, 48.

[8]*Mos.* ii, 52.

extremely subtle, but quite basic. For to the rabbis the Torah existed eternally as a collection of individual laws, while to Philo, like the Greeks, the Law which was eternally existent was the essentially singular Logos of Nature or of God and had plural manifestation only as it represented itself in the material of nouns and verbs, just as the Idea of Beauty became plural for Plato only in its material manifestations. So as Plato desired to rise from beauties to Beauty, Philo saw the laws of the Torah as chiefly important for leading him beyond them to the Law of God and Nature. This contrast and ambition distinguishes Philo from the rabbis who almost universally (I know no exceptions but, not being a rabbinist, have not in mind every possible passage) saw the heavenly Torah itself as a collection of Laws, in which each "jot" and "tittle", that is not only every word but every letter and every ornamental stroke on every letter, was eternally existent and sacred.[9] Wolfson has changed Philo's statement to make him too speak of the eternal laws, and so to make him conform to rabbinic thinking,

A similar difficulty arises (II, 201) when Wolfson discusses Philo's notion that the ten commandments underlie all the specific laws as their basic principles, the primary and most miraculous formulations of the Law behind all the laws. As a parallel Wolfson refers to the *Canticles Rabbah,* which, like all these midrashim, has early material, but which was completed almost certainly not earlier than the sixth century. Since Wolfson does not demonstrate that his particular quotation here is from an early date, we must assume that it is, if not the latest thing in the work, at least centuries later than Philo. Yet, simply with reference to the *Canticles Rabbah* Wolfson says: "in rabbinic literature, it is similarly said that the ten commandments contain all the laws of the Torah. This last method of classification is adopted by Philo." A few lines below he speaks of the "traditional origin" of religion's method of classifying the "special laws" under one or another of the ten commandments. The reader unaware of the dates of the rabbinic material would naturally suppose that Wolfson has indicted the source of Philo's ideas. The reader who is aware of the dates wonders what Wolfson can be thinking about to write in this way.

Wolfson is sure that Philo's allegorical interpretation had its inspiration in "native Jewish tradition." He begins (I, 115-131) by saying that, like the rabbis, however much Philo might read into Scripture he never gave up a sense of the value of its literal meaning: with which every student of Philo would at once agree. It is true, Wolfson goes on (I, 131-133), that Greeks had allegorized their Homer, Hesiod, and other sources of mythology, though with this Philo could have had no sympathy because he so completely rejected Greek mythology. "But what he denies to mythology he claims for the divinely revealed Hebrew Scripture" (I, 133). Up to this point Wolfson seems to be going along with the rest of us in seeing Philo's allegory heavily indebted to the

---

[9]G. F. Moore, *Judaism* (1927-1930), I, 269 f.; III, 83.

Greeks. Then he begins to point out that the rabbis too hedged at the anthropomorphic expressions about God in the Scriptures, that they tempered the naivete of many statements in the historical narratives of the Torah, and frequently in truth abrogated the letter of specific laws by their interpretations to adapt them to later society. "This is the conception of Scripture with which Philo started," Wolfson says (I, 138), where we would still agree, even though some of the parallels in interpreting specific laws which Wolfson quotes between Philo and the rabbis do not seem to establish that Philo had his interpretation of the laws from rabbis of the "native" school. Let us admit that Philo did not have to learn from the Greeks that there were many awkward passages in the Torah which had to be explained away. *The real problem is where he learned that he had not the true meaning of Scripture until he had a meaning in harmony with Greek categories of thought and mysticism.* This central problem Wolfson barely skirts.

This allegorizing of myths was in Greek tradition especially the work of the hellenistic and later centuries. Another product of the same period, one which has been completely documented as pagan from many sources and many scholars, is the notion of the radiance of God's nature which manifested itself as the Logos when considered as a unit, but as Powers when considered for the plural impact of the radiation. In more popular religious circles these Powers became descending pairs of mythical personalities. Rejecting of course the mythical personalities, it has generally been supposed that Philo shows this pagan doctrine in Jewish dress in his passages on the Logos and the Powers. Wolfson disagrees for several reasons, the chief being that to him both the Logos and the Powers are Jewish created beings rather than pagan emanations. In arguing that Philo's Logos was created (I, 234 ff.) he admits that Philo never said so, but makes that inference none the less from several of Philo's statements. "The Logos is thus spoken of as the eldest and most generic of created things," he begins, quite overtranslating Philo's πρεσβύτατος καὶ γενικώτατος τῶν ὅσα γέγονε,[10] which means "eldest and most generic of the things which came into existence," without reference one way or the other to their being created. Other phases which imply to Wolfson that the Logos was created are: "'older than all things which are the object of creation,' as not being uncreated as God, though not created as human beings, as being the first-born son of God, the man of God, the image of God, second to God, a second God, and as being called a god by those who have an imperfect knowledge of the real God" (I, 234). Wolfson continues to refer to more passages of the sort, not one of which proves his point. He admits an eternal Logos, but only as the mind of God, as which it is "something identical with the essence of God" (I, 231). But in its usual sense of a manifestation in some way to be distinguished from God it is "something created by God" (I, 239). So when Philo talks of the Logos and

---

[10]LA, iii, 175.

Powers as "growing out" or coming from a "source," Wolfson feels that he can say finally, we must not hink of emanations (I, 237).

Wolfson has an excellent passage (I, 261 ff.) discussing Philo's relation to Aristotle on the ground that Philo makes the Logos the ὄργανον of God in creation. In contrast Sophia is not the ὄργανον but the "mother and nurse" (I, 266 ff.), Wolfson says, for these are terms which in other passages Philo applies to matter as contrasted with form. Philo could not have had this, Wolfson assures us, from the Egyptian and the Greek mystic notion of Mother Earth, the mother and nurse of us all, which such men as Plutarch explained as being the material, or the universal feminine, principle. Wolfson does not discuss this evidence, for Philo "undoubtedly" (I, 269) got it by reading the Hebrew אמן now as *artisan* (אָמָן), now as *nurse* (אֹמֵן), and now as *their mother* (אָמָן) (I, 267 f.). This is *pilpul* with distinction! To the sexual imagery with which Philo discusses the relation of God and Sophia Wolfson alludes only in a footnote of two lines (I, 266).

One could go on with this sort of thing indefinitely. In reading the book I early came to keep a red pencil at hand and mark those places where Wolfson ties Philo back to "native Jewish tradition." Both volumes are studded with red. But Wolfson's parallels in almost no case have any justification to pose as the "source" of Philo. That Philo must have had much in common with rabbinic tradition no one in his senses would deny, or that the solution of what that relationship was is one of the most important problems of Philonic study. Throughout my own writing I have often lamented my lack of rabbinic training, and so my incompetence to deal with the question. I have accordingly never tried to write a comprehensive work on Philo because I have felt that without a solution to the rabbinic variable the formula of Philo's thinking could not be solved. In trying to prove too much, and in his uncritical use of rabbinic sources, Wolfson has only confused the matter more deeply. So far as this matter is concerned the thesis seems to be his statement (I, 56): "Alexandrian Judaism at the time of Philo [it was Philo who brought it to full development, he said (I, 95)] was a collateral branch of Pharisaic Judaism, which flourished in Palestine at that time, both of them having sprung from that pre-Maccabean Judaism which had been molded by the activities of the Scribes." The basic confusion of Wolfson's thought is well expressed here. Wolfson says not that Alexandrian and Pharisaic Judaism were collateral branches descended from a single Jewish original, to which no one could object; but that Alexandrian Judaism was a branch of Pharisaic Judaism because both had a common ancestor. This is to say that my cousin is my father because we have a common grandfather. The statement would be only a meaningless and amusing solecism such as we all make frequently if its confusion did not represent the confusion of the book as a whole. For the impression Wolfson makes abundantly is that he believes that in the writings of rabbinic Judaism, even quite late Judaism, we can find the source of Philo's thinking: not the direct source, for Philo had never read the *Mekilta,* but still the ideas with which Philo was working. Whenever there is a similarity it could never be a coincidence, or the influence of hellenized thinking on the rabbis, but only something which Philo had from the rabbis themselves. This is true however remote the similarity. To such a thesis we must simply say "non probatur."

A final word on methodology. Wolfson protests (I, 106 f.) that it is not enough in studying a thinker of the past to collect related passages from his writings and arrange them under headings, with comparison to similar passages in other philosophers and the Bible, but that we must try to reconstruct the latent processes of the man's reasoning and to determine the true meaning of what is said by seeing how he came to say it. But if we may add the rabbinic writings to the philosophers and the Bible, this rejected method is exactly that of Wolfson. He takes related passages of Philo from all his works (without reference to their contexts there, or the character of the different writings), finds parallels in a rabbinic source or in Plato, Aristotle, or the Stoics, and shows how the statements of Philo might have been made if he had had the passages from the other sources "clearly in mind" as he wrote. As to whether Philo did have those sources "clearly in mind" Wolfson never seems to doubt, if by them he can explain a passage. By such a method we can make individual passages mean about what we please: actually the only control, beside such mechanical matters as caution about the dates of material one treats as a source, is integration. How do our conclusions about details fit into the man's work as a whole?

Oddly Wolfson's statement on methodology does not mention integration. The total picture of the man, let's call him Philo again, can only be either a pattern we impose upon him or the pattern of Philo himself. Actually we all come out with a compromise, one where our subjective notions have come at best only more or less to reflect those of religion himself. That is what I meant when I said in another connection that the study of Philo, or any other philosopher, will always be a spiral approaching Philo as a limit. But what I insist is that much as we must always try to understand fragmentary statements of Philo by reference to "parallels" or "sources" of one sort or another, in constructing the totality we must follow large consecutive blocks of Philo's thinking and actual presentation, rather than blocks and headings of our own construction. In the series of writings commonly called the "Exposition of the Law" Philo develops a great thesis which begins with the foundation of Law (not laws) in the creation of the universe, and goes on to the incarnate representation of this Law in the Patriarchs, each of whom is a νόμος ἔμψυχος; then to the miraculous formation of Law verbally as laws, first in the decalogue and then secondarily, using these as principles, in the individual laws of the Torah. Philo has throughout concentrated upon the fact that these verbal laws, as general principles or as derivative laws, complied with the basic Moral Principle of the universe which metaphysically he expressed in the terms Logos or Sophia as he had learned them from the Greeks. So at the end of the "Exposition" Philo returns to review this, to discuss the fact that the true Jew (true nobility) is one who, gentile or Jew by birth, understands and observes the Jewish Law with this sense of its implications in mind. Philo closes the work by discussing the rewards and punishments of this legal system.

It is curious that to this great work of Philo, made up of many treatises, Wolfson never once alludes as a whole, and this integration of Philo's thought, which is as near Philo's integration as I think we can ever get, Wolfson never discusses. The problem of Philo's relation to rabbinic Judaism and Greek philosophy is not to be solved by splitting his atoms, but by understanding his integration, and the same may be said of understanding Philo himself, only for Philo as the confluence of Judaism and Greek critical philosophy, and so as the keystone in his construction of the history of European philosophy. Wolfson has written a great *tour de force* in taking so many fragments of Philo and making them fit into a preconceived notion of Philo and his place in history. No one hereafter may write on a passage in Philo without first seeing whether Wolfson has discussed it and what he has to say about it, especially for the relation of the passage to classical philosophy. The book should be called *A Philonic System*, for this it is. The mistake is to call it simply *Philo*, for I found little of Philo himself or his spirit in it.

Chapter Seven

Jewish Symbolism

Encyclopedia Judaica (Jerusalem, 1971), 15:568-578

A peculiar phenomenon occurred during the centuries when Jewish tradition was being formulated in the Talmud and Midrash. As modern archaeologists uncovered Jewish graves, funerary objects, and synagogues of that period (in large numbers), they found on them various animals and human figures, as well as vines and other pagan forms, in painting, mosaic, relief, and, in a few cases, in the round. These appear on Jewish remains from Tunisia to Italy and eastward to the Euphrates. In Palestine, where the remains are more abundant, what were aberrations from the point of view of later rabbinic tradition are almost omnipresent.

The material, itself indisputable, has caused considerable disagreement. Could these be called symbols at all; or, as has been repeatedly suggested, do they show only that Jews were "rather lax" at the time in borrowing ornament, and that the figures in no case indicate an ideological invasion of Judaism from the pagan world? One commentator explicitly said that the new discoveries must not be allowed to disrupt the picture of Judaism in the first Christian centuries as it has traditionally been reconstructed from rabbinic writings.

Such reasoning seems to lie behind the statement of N. Avigad *(Israel Exploration Journal,* 7 (1957), 252 ff.) about a Helios (sun god) head on a sarcophagus found in a catacomb at Bet She'arim, where rabbinic families were buried. He says that "it can be presumed" that neither the craftsman nor the purchaser had any knowledge of the original meaning of Helios. He goes on to suggest that it had by this time lost all meaning, and indeed that the various pagan representations borrowed by Jews had lost all their "original symbolic significance." This can indeed apply to the single Helios head in the catacomb. However, Helios appears at the center of five of the synagogue floors found in Palestine, and various sun-god symbols with Jewish labels are upon numerous amulets of the time. The question whether Helios had lost all significance in the third century for pagans, and was borrowed by Jews only for decoration cannot, then, be dismissed with hasty presumptions.

The symbols borrowed from paganism often appear on monuments inextricably mingled with representations of objects used in Jewish worship: the *lulav* and *etrog,* the *shofar,* the Ark of the Law, and, most commonly of all, the *menorah*, almost always with seven branches. There is also surprisingly often what is unmistakably an incense burner. At a time when pagans often put cult symbols on their graves, and when Christians were beginning universally to bury their dead with a cross or other Christian symbol in the hope of immortality, the Jews of the period probably used their own symbols to express a similar hope. There is a *menorah* with birds eating grapes on either side of it. Birds eating grapes certainly symbolized immortality to Christians, and probably to pagans as well, so that it is hard to believe that the birds and grapes were not also as symbolic to Jews as were the *menorot*. It is still harder to believe that such a design was scratched on a stone in the eternal darkness of a Roman catacomb merely for decorative purposes.

Conclusions can be formed, however, not by speculating about individual examples, but by studying the entire phenomenon. From the description of Solomon's Temple and from the denunciations of the prophets it is clear that Jews had begun using symbols (or decorations) for their places of worship in very early times. However, except for occasional Palestinian seals, only literary reports of such use of forms survive. During roughly the century between 50 years before and 50 years after the common era, a number of geometrical symbols, mostly rosettes, columns, conventionalized flowers, and zigzag lines, were put on many of the ossuaries used at that time for the final interment of bones. These symbols and vines were also put over the entrances to tombs or on their doors. So many of the coffers have Jewish names scratched on them that no one doubts the Jewish origin of most of them, though perhaps some may have been Jewish Christian. Except for a very few with wine cups, Jewish cult objects never appear on these receptacles, and why the Jews of that time used the geometrical figures cannot be established, though this does not mean that they were necessarily meaningless decoration.

Some 30 or 40 years after the devastation of the Bar Kokhba war, the graves and synagogues of Palestine, and the graves of Rome, suddenly began to present new designs. This occurred even in Tiberias, Palestine, where the rabbinical academy reached its height and its greatest authority.

Common Symbols. Among the Jewish symbols it is difficult to judge whether the seven-branched *menorah* or the Ark of the Law representing the Law itself had the greater importance. The *menorah* appears much more often, but when the two are shown together the Ark is always central. The group has been found in synagogues at Bet Alfa and Dura Europos and in burial designs at Bet She'arim. It is also found, to name only a few instances, on gold glasses in Rome, and in the lunettes of two arcosolia (space for a sarcophagus) in a Roman catacomb. On Roman remains it is often combined with wine symbols. The ritualistic use of bread and wine, especially the latter, has never been lost from Jewish life, so that grapes, cups, and vines, on synagogues and graves, and even as part of the special cluster of ritual symbols, commonly appear. These suggest that wine had a more important share in the hope of immortality than apparently associated with the other symbols than one would suspect from medieval Orthodox writings.

It is accordingly very interesting that without any association with the cult objects, the vine and cup symbols appear so universally in synagogue art. A vine with loops, more or less conventionalized, was depicted in a great many synagogues with various symbols represented inside the loops, such as found in the borders at Bet Alfa and Meron in Israel, and Hammam Lif in Tunisia. At Chorazin in Israel a series of Dionysiac vintage scenes appears in such loops, and in the Dura Europos synagogue the paintings are all set within vine borders above the Dionysiac masks and felines of the dado. The most important scene in this synagogue shows a great vine which grows up to a throne high up at the top, and which, with a figure of Orpheus and his lyre, seems to take the tribes of Israel up to that throne. Thus, wine symbols run from the simple cups and birds eating grapes to Dura's elaborate presentation of salvation in terms of the vine. In any other body of religious remains, such evidence would be "presumed" to indicate great religious value in the ceremonial drinking of wine. "Presumption" is a world that can never be used with Jewish material: but if Jews were depicting wine symbols in a way that would indicate religious meaning in the symbolism of other religions, the most likely hypothesis is that wine had religious meaning for the Jews who used the symbols, even though there are not literary remains to indicate the significance in words. It is necessary to consider whether the symbols were at this time dead in paganism, as Avigad asserted. This has long been the position of Catholic scholars. They hold that early Christian sacramentalism and hope of immortality was able to express itself in pagan symbols because the pagan forms, however symbolic originally, had become quite meaningless devices for decoration by the time Christians took them over and gave them Christian meaning. The theory was formed by churchmen long before they knew that Jews had also borrowed the same symbols, and it was always a mere assertion, never investigated at all. The existing evidence, even with all the literary material that could be used with the representations, does not remotely justify the churchmen's assertions that the pagans used the forms simply as decorative devices. Conspicuously, the Jewish usages occurred mostly from the third to the sixth centuries, the very years when, for Christians at least, such forms as the wine symbols were being used with the most obvious reverence and meaning. Since Christians began their pictorial art largely by borrowing and adapting a Jewish tradition of Old Testament art, it may well have been Jews who began the adaptation of Dionysiac symbols for their Jewish ritual, after which Christians took them over for their Eucharist, which itself seems an adaptation of the *Kiddush*. Whichever of the two religions began the adapting, the height of Jewish usage coincided exactly with the height of Christian usage, so that it is difficult to suggest that Jews were using forms which at that time had no meaning.

Pagan Devices. The forms on Jewish amulets at the time show the great concern of Jews with pagan devices. What are known as amulets may have been worn with no more meaning than that which people today wear birth stones and ancient coins or scarabs. But the ancient amulets bear much more inherent likeness to religious "medals," as they are now called, objects worn by no means for decoration. Some amulets may have become as elaborate and decorative as a bishop's cross, but no one would think that this detracted from the cross's direct religious significance. Many of the ancient amulets are designs stamped on worthless metal, things neither of beauty nor of monetary value. If the designs can appear on such cheap, ugly articles or on valuable stones indiscriminately, clearly the value of the medium and the skill of execution bear no relation to the value of the device itself. Those who could not put the designs on valuable stones had to put them on their little medals, because it must be inferred, what really mattered was the design. The most common devices are those that seem solar in their reference: the snake-footed warrior usually with a cock's head (the anguiped), but sometimes with a lion's head or driving a quadriga. The lion appears often, probably always as solar, for it was frequently drawn as the head of the Chnoubis snake. These are only a few of the snake types that in general, by reason of the names used with them, seem to be of Jewish origin.

Addresses to Iao with the varient name of Helios appear in the chants or charms: "Hail Helios, hail Helios, hail Gabriel, hail Rapael, hail Michael ... Give me the authority and power of Sabaoth, the strength of Iao," etc. More than 200 such addresses can be quoted. This makes it more and more difficult to accept Avigad's "presumption" that Helios must have been a meaningless figure on the sarcophagus and in the synagogue. The lion on amulets suggests the many lions on synagogue floors and on sarcophagi, where they face cups, hold victims, guard the Torah, or are tamed by the music of Orpheus. The felines at Dura Europos, represented with Orpheus, with the crater, and with masks, recall the Dionysiac lion, as familiar a figure as the solar lion. Jews seem to have borrowed the lion, or felines in general, with either of these associations. Felines appear so often on pagan and Jewish sarcophagi that they would seem to be another of the symbols of immortality.

The eagle, which was especially hateful in Jewish eyes, also occurs with great frequency. The earliest known instance is the golden eagle on Herod's temple. As Herod was dying, some fanatics gave their lives to tear down the eagle, though it had apparently been there a long time, and the fanatics were disavowed by the Jewish populace. But eagles were carved on several Jewish stones in the Crimea, and in the sudden burst of decorated synagogues at the end of the second century, eagles were often carved, usually, as in the Crimea, in connection with wreaths. Eagles appear at each end of the great stone table that stood like a Christian alter before the apse of the synagogue at Sardis.

There were many other borrowed symbols; the tree, the shell, figures of Victory (usually also bearing crowns or wreaths), masks of the sort usually associated with Dionysus as cult instruments to hang on trees or to display in initiations, bundles of grain or grapes or pomegranates, the head of the "ubiquitous Demeter-Persephone of the eastern Mediterranean," shown many times in the tiles and dado of the Dura synagogue and once in mosaic at the Jaffa bull and vucrania (ox head), Medusa heads, cupids, cocks, peacocks, boats, adders, and a number of other symbols, including the zodiac and the four seasons – one has only to list them to see that the motifs Jews borrowed fall into a rather closely associated group. Almost all were taken over by Christians at the same time to symbolize their hope of immortality and God's loving mercy in giving it to the devout. Put upon their graves, the symbols helped Christians get into heaven, as does the cross today, although there is no formal doctrinal declaration that it does so. During life, the symbols seem to have had power to bring deity to the devout – both Christians and Dionysiac ecstatics – perhaps just for protection, perhaps with a sense of the real presence with which mysticism begins.

The issue comes sharply to a head in the synagogue at Hammath-Tiberias. In this locality several synagogues were built successively on the same site, but the one in use at the time when the rabbinic Sanhedrin was centered there not only had painted walls but also a large mosaic floor in three panels, as at Bet Alfa. One panel shows a similar presentation of Jewish cult objects, while the central one is occupied by a Helios driving his chariot within a circle of the zodiac. Helios has "an aureole surrounding his head, one hand raised in blessing, and the other holding the sphere of the heavens." The figures in the zodiac are naked. Female busts in the corners have the names of the seasons in Hebrew, but the third panel has a Greek donor's inscription flanked by lions. How the rabbis of the Sanhedrin regarded such art, or what relation they had personally to the synagogue, is a matter of pure speculation. The donor's title, "Severus, servant of the illustrious presidents," has been suggested to mean that Severus was a high official in the court of the presidents of the Sanhedrin in Tiberias, leading to the conclusion that the founders of the synagogue were closely connected with the Sanhedrin. But close relations with such art would never have been guessed from the recorded writings of the rabbis themselves. The relation, let alone its implication, is by no means so well attested that it may be concluded merely from it that Helios and the rest had lost all meaning for those Jews who ordered such synagogue mosaics. One can only conclude that if Severus was really in such high standing with the great rabbis of Hammath, it is as likely that they had ideas in accord with the symbols as that the symbols were meaningless in Jewish usage.

Meaning. Here is the heart of the problem: what did such devices mean to the Jews using them? In the Dura Europos synagogue many of these same devices were put directly into scenes painted to represent and interpret biblical incidents. Such extensive borrowings in any other religion would at once be taken to indicate a direct adoption of the symbolic value. Does the complete absence of any corresponding symbolic reference in the rabbinic writings that have come down to us warrant an a priori premise that the forms could not have had such meaning in popular Judaism? If they had any meaning at all they presumably show that Jews at the time were much more concerned than the recorded rabbis with Hellenistic mystic hopes of immortality, hopes that they believed would be fulfilled by their Jewish God, but hopes that in form, at least, much resembled those of the mystery cults.

The symbols by no means present the first appearance of such an invasion of Hellenistic religiosity into Judaism. Any student of Philo's writings and of the fragments of Hellenized Judaism knows that the Judaism in them has been deeply affected by the religious aspirations, which pagans expressed in the terminology of the mystic religions and philosophies. The Jewish documents, in fact, used the same language to describe the religious values of Judaism. This ran over into a Jewish gnosticism and mysticism in which there is no reason to doubt that Jews who seem as loyal to Jewish legal observances as was apparently Philo himself, found their deepest satisfaction in kinds of religious conceptions which have made him unpopular with "rabbinic" Jews from his own day to the present. Some scholars have regarded Philo as a loyal Jew with a Greek veneer, a veneer which had great importance for the development of Christianity, but none for the development of Judaism itself. This was the attitude of G.F. Moore, as elaborated by H.A. Wolfson. But for the most part the history of Jewish mysticism has been expounded, by such outstanding scholars as G. Scholem, with no reference to Philo or Hellenism at all.

Philo makes no allusion to images except to express typical Jewish scorn of their worship. There is no evidence to suggest that he ever used any of the pagan symbols that archaeology shows Jews to have used soon after his time. What he does reveal, however, is that ideas of religious objectives, types of religious formulations and experiences, could be appropriated as the objectives of Judaism, the meaning of biblical revelation, and that the pagan mystic vocabulary could be adopted to explain the meaning of the Torah itself. Archaeology shows that soon after Philo, Jews could use the language of pagan symbols in their most sacred places – places of worship and of burial. Did Jews use them merely to ape the pagans with decorative devices, or because the devices had a value which they thought they could find in their Torah?

There are two levels of syncretism, or religious mixing. To illustrate the contrast in Christian language, one type could have said, for example, that Jesus is identical with Orpheus, and that worship of Orpheus was actually worship of Jesus. Such actual identification of divine persons seems to be the syncretism of the *Hermetica* and the Gnostics. The other would say that the experience which pagans described as having been given them in Orphic rites was really given to Christians in Jesus. Without any recognition of pagan divine persons, that is, the second type of syncretism appropriates the religious experiences of others and finds them through its own divine persons or Person, though still using the old symbols, Gandhi did this when he adopted much of the Judeo-Christian tradition while remaining a loyal Hindu. Philo did so with much in Greek tradition while remaining a loyal Jew. The prophets and rabbis who denounced the gods of the Caananites came to claim for their own God the Caananite seasonal festivals, and, possibly, much of Canaanite ritual.

Symbols and religious experiences and values have a way of disengaging themselves from their original mythical explanations and going from religion to religion with the old forms and values now given new explanations. One sees this in the cup. Apart from the general history of divine fluid, the wine of Dionysus in some way continues as the wine of the Christian Eucharist. In both, the god or God is the vine, is the grape, is the wine, and in drinking it the believer gets "enthusiasm," the god in him, and in both it is the "medicine of immortality." Christianity told new stories about a new name for this, and Christians would suffer torture to the death, like good Jews, rather than "drink of the cup of demons," the cup of Dionysus and his syncretistic fellows like Sabazius. But by new explanations the old cup, still on their graves, was the Christians' cup. It was at the very time that all this was most meaningfully being done by Christians that Jews were also putting cups and other wine symbols on their graves and in their synagogues, Jews of whom nothing whatever is known but their archaeological remains. There is every reason to believe that Jews had long been blessing their wine cups and using them to consecrate Sabbaths, festivals, weddings, and circumcisions. The only possible conclusion, and this an unlikely one, is that Jews of the Roman world were the only ones to whom the ritualistic drinking of wine was merely a convention of obedience.

The Jews seem to have taken over other symbols from paganism in much the same way, but each must be traced in detail for every example of it in the early religions, as well as its use in Christianity. It gradually appears that the Jews were not adapting random forms, but a language, a subverbal language of the emotions which could be used to express the hopes and achievements of any eschatological or mystical religion. This subverbal language, like all emotional expression, cannot be translated into words. The nearest verbal language is that of the mystic, who uses words for the richness of their emotional impact rather than for any precise denotation.

Mystic Symbolism in Judaism. In the modern obsessively verbal civilization scholars find it hard to understand the language of symbolism and its reality for almost all ancient peoples. Symbolic words are in use today, such as "love," "liberty," "patriotism," "justice," and people live by them in their largely undefined richness. A sense of security comes from them and from the emotions they arouse and stabilize; for such words millions have willingly died. But most of the soldiers and social workers who give their lives for them have little use for the orators who expound them. Symbols of form and ritual work in the same way. The cross or the Torah scroll itself has much more reality for the believer than the explanations priests or rabbis can give it. Also, new groups can take over other people's symbols and give them new verbal associations while they prize them for the old values. It is not possible yet to say whether the approach here suggested for symbols is adequate or even valid, since it has been so newly proposed. At best it will establish only a probability, but the probability must come from the art itself, along with any written documents that may come to light; but even if a written statement should appear from a Jew of those centuries describing the symbols, there would be a danger of too hasty generalization. The statement of any one person about what the terms "love" or "patriotism" mean to him could hardly go straight into a dictionary as the general meaning of the words. The fact now is that for the meaning of the symbols there are only the symbols themselves.

Granted for the moment that as mystic ideas went into Hellenistic Judaism with the Greek mystic vocabulary, so the mystic symbols took their mystic hopes with them to the Jews who adopted them. It would then appear that from Rome and Tunisia through Asia Minor and Palestine and eastward to the Euphrates, the Judaism of the great majority of Jews would have been a basically mystic Judaism, in form if not in individual achievement. But that such a Judaism could have existed will surprise no one who has read the writings of G. Scholem or the text of Philo. If such a mystic Judaism existed as extensively as do the symbols in Jewish remains, however, what became of it, why did it so largely disappear, or, since mystic Judaism never ceased to exist, why did Jews abandon the symbols to express it?

For this question a few facts must be mentioned from which argument can proceed.

(1) The great period of borrowing seems to have been from the end of the second through the fourth century C.E., the period when the Jews were least threatened by gentile society. By the fifth and sixth centuries the now dominant Christians were showing much less tolerance of Jewish practices than had the Romans, and animosity between Jews and Christians had deepened.

(2) It was not until the beginning of the sixth century that the Talmud was completed, if it can be said ever to have been completed. At least it was C. 400 C.E. that the *Gemara* was codified to go with the Mishnah.

(3) The great majority of Jews, even the leaders of communities, had for centuries spoken Greek or, later, Latin in the West but still largely Greek even in Palestine. By the third century B.C.E. the Septuagint translation was begun, and when Christian interpretations made this text awkward in places and Jews disavowed it, the rabbis were nevertheless aware that those in the Diaspora, at least, had to have a Bible they could read, and so authorized other translations, especially that of Aquila. But since the Mishnah always remained in Hebrew, a language no longer spoken outside the academies, it would have been quite unintelligible generally, even to the great majority of Jews in Palestine.

(4) The Talmud and Midrashim present an almost unbroken condemnation of any image-making for Jewish use (though craftsmen were permitted to make images for pagans). Rabbinical students have ever since understood that borrowing pagan figures for ornament was as little permitted as for idolatry, since idolatry seemed always possible with any image. The rabbis as finally reported associated even an emperor's image on a coin with possible idolatry.

(5) In the sixth and seventh centuries great iconoclastic movements swept the Western and Near Eastern world and registered deeply in the new Islam and in much of Christianity. It was at this time, as 19th-century archaeologists already recognized, that Jews not only stopped making decorations but began chipping them off the synagogues still in use. For this it is interesting to see a drawing of the lintel of the main entrance of the synagogue at Capernaum, where festooned loops, rosettes, and two trees of life are left, while a row of cupids that supported the festoons and a spread eagle below them have been cut away. (For further examples see Goodenough, *Symbols* ... vol. 3. figs. 460f., 465, 489, 491, 497, 510-2, 525, 644, where eagles, Victories, lions, zodiac signs, Helios, and other living creatures were cut away, while the "harmless" designs were left.) These stones show such selective defacements that the people who mutilated them clearly intended to remove only what was offensive and to leave the buildings still usable. This might have been done by later Muslims, but the experts who examined the stones have long agreed that it was probably Jews who did so. Since an eagle or lion would be cut away from one building and left on another, it is to be presumed that the reaction against images was sporadic and affected some congregations earlier than others, while some buildings collapsed with their ornament still intact. But there can be no dispute that those who originally erected the images were thinking differently from those who cut them down. Where formerly they were desired by some and tolerated by all (though for what reason is precisely the matter in dispute), they had now become offensive.

(6) At about this time, perhaps a century later, another change took place in Rome and Italy generally. Whereas the Jews in the West spoke Greek or Latin, used these languages with the images on their tombs, and presumably read their Torah and prayed in Greek, suddenly, in about the seventh or eighth century, these languages entirely disappeared and Hebrew took over. Something had happened that taught Roman Jews that the true language of their religion was Hebrew, and even made them learn to use that language. Changing a people's language indeed indicates a revolution in its thinking.

(7) From this time on, Jews of Western Europe worshiped in Hebrew and considered the Babylonian Talmud almost as authoritative literature, and in attitude toward figured decoration. The facts must all be considered together. Any reconstruction of what lay behind them must be conjectural, but they suggest the following. Jews seem to have been much influenced by pagan mystical thinking in the Greco-Roman world, so that, however much their lost

writings may have expressed the mystic Judaism that resulted, they expressed it also in the subverbal language of the symbols. Many rabbis did not like this, and their view eventually prevailed, so that not only did the image-making stop, but as far as possible the images still visible were "annulled" by being defaced. The aniconic opinion prevailed, partly because the Jews shared in current iconoclasm, and partly because the conservative rabbis, who kept to the *halakhah*, offered the Jews religion whose base was not the mysticism and allegory of Christianity, but an orthopraxy that refused to use such figures as Orpheus, since these now generally expressed the ideals and aims of their Christian oppressors. It is possible that it was at this time that what G.F. Moore called "normative Judaism" did at last become normative, but that mystic Judaism, though it gave up the images, survived in popular Jewish usage, to reappear centuries later as Kabbalah, by which time it had been much influenced by later mystic writers of Islam and Christianity. Whether this guess is right or wrong cannot be determined until scholars examine the Zohar and its cognates with Philo and the Greco-Roman Jewish symbols in mind. Methodologically, however, it may be remarked that differences between earlier Hellenized Jewish mysticism and the much later Kabbalah will of course often appear, but these will not cancel impressions of continuity which similarities that have survived a millennium will suggest.

One last question remains. What was the relation of all this symbolic Judaism to the rabbis? Unless the question is brushed aside by denying that there was any "symbolic Judaism" and admitting only a wide laxity in the use of meaningless ornament, the question presents difficulties. One solution has been to find fragmentary statements of tolerance in rabbinic writings. It has been urged that today's conception of rabbinic aniconism is much exaggerated, since some rabbis allowed Jewish craftsmen to make images for pagans, even though the Jews knew that the pagans would use them as idols. But this has no relevance whatever in explaining why Jews put images into their synagogues and graves, since these were made "for themselves," exactly the distinction on which the craftsmen were allowed to make images for others. A few passages have been found where rabbis "did not object" to the images even in synagogues, but these by no means counterbalance the thunderous denunciations of images in general in the tannaitic Midrashim and the *Avodah Zarah*. It is not occasional tolerance that will explain this art, but motivation for its being so widely borrowed, and this motivation appears in not a single rabbinic passage.

The use of such art, together with the discovery of new mystic treatises by G. Scholem, makes it possible to question whether the rabbinic writings which survive adequately represent the variety of thought among the rabbis themselves. The ideas of the rabbis who produced the mystic books, of which even Scholem has probably found only a very small part, are suggested in the rabbinic texts only by rare and veiled allusions. If these symbols speak a language foreign to "rabbinic" Judaism, they may not be at all foreign to the religion of many rabbis whose points of view "rabbinic" Judaism, as it finally crystalized in the written tradition, did not see fit to preserve. For it seems entirely possible that defenders of the halakhic "rabbinic" Judaism expunged mystic Judaism from the writings as drastically as did those who chiseled the offensive forms from the synagogues, though there is no proof that any such expurgation of rabbinic writings occurred. What all or some rabbis may have thought about this art, however, is quite secondary to its existence, and the necessity to understand it in its own right.

Bibliography

E.R. Goodenough, *Jewish Symbols in the Greco-Roman Period*, 12 vols. (1953-65); H. Kohl and O. Watzinger, *Antike Synagogen in Galilaea* (1916); E.L. Sukenik, *Ancient Synagogues in Palestine and Greece* (1934); idem. *Ancient Synagogue of Beth Alpha* (1932); H.W. Beyer and H. Lietzmann, *Juedische Denkmaeler* (1930)

Chapter Eight

The Evaluation of Symbols Recurrent in Time, As Illustrated in Judaism

Eranos-Jahrbuch 1951, 20-285-319

The problem which I shall present is one at the core of a large investigation. Before stating the problem itself I must tell briefly of the investigation.

The discovery of the synagogue at Dura Europos startled the world, because the world had long been ignoring the accumulating evidence that in the Greco-Roman period Jews had widely used an art which in itself looked highly syncretistic, one in which the divine figures of the Pagans, and many of their most important religious symbols, were used with the greatest freedom in Jewish tombs and synagogues. This syncretistic art of Judaism had basically the vocabulary of early Christian symbolism as well, but that fact had impressed few who dealt with early Christian art, for they, for the most part, had gone on saying that of course, since Jewish law forbade it, Jews had had no art. Furthermore historians of art had utterly failed to see the implications of the ideas of Stzygowsky as elaborated by Mory of Princeton, that all early Christian illustrations of the Old Testament seem explicable only if the Christians who made them had been adapting a tradition of Old Testament art originally developed by Jews, presumably in Alexandria. As a result of this general ignoring of indications of a Jewish art, the historians of religion and art were completely bewildered when the Dura synagogue was discovered, its wall painted with Old Testament scenes in a way that showed collateral descent from the hypothetical ancestors of the O.T. illustrations of the Hexateuchs, and of Santa Maria Maggiore in Rome, and when with these were presentations of Bacchic vines, Orpheus playing to the animals, Bacchic felines and masks, winged victories, and the god Ares, as well as the three nymphs, the divine nurses of the young gods, here as nurses of the infant Moses. They should not have been bewildered at all, for such a discovery was only the next step, the laboratory confirmation of the best thinking and the culmination of the discoveries of long before in synagogues and Jewish graves. The uncovering of the extraordinary Jewish catacombs at Sheikh Ibreik in Galilee two years later was less publicized, but was of equal importance.

If historians of art were amazed at such confirmation of the best theory of the background of Christian art forms, historians of religion have been even more incredulous at what has appeared. Ready at once to conclude syncretism when an Osirian mummy portrait shows the person holding a dionysiac wine cup, or when Orpheus is presented within a Zocias, or a Palmyrian figure in trousers lies carved in his tomb on a dionysiac couch of immortality, we had all been trained to believe that syncretism was a word we could never use of the Jews, trained so well that even when on the mosaic floors of three synagogues in Palestine Helios was found driving his chariot within the circle of the zodiac, no one thought to suggest that here was syncretism quite as obviously as in the pagan cases. Indeed one of the Jewish archeologists and historians of art most active in presenting this Jewish material said that it had all along been a mistake to suggest that representations of the vine in either Christianity or paganism could have had symbolic meaning, since the vine and cup were used extensively by Jews in the period, and hence must have been purely decorative everywhere.

Such a statement is only the epitome of general rejection of symbolic interpretation for this Jewish art, but interestingly enough it puts the issue squarely before us at last. For Avi-Yonah, who said it, recognized, at least unconsciously, that there could be no double standard: that the use of such symbols by pagans, Jews, and Christians must all be considered on a level. If the art forms were symbolic with one group, they must have been so with all. That Avi-Yonah had consciously elaborated such a theory for his quite off-hand statement cannot be assumed. But many times our off-hand statements are more important than our elaborated formulations, and such is the case here.

For the real question is put to us directly by Avi-Yonah: the art of the period, pagan, Jewish, and Christian, must be considered together, insofar, at least, as each presents us with the same forms as the others. What we need, however, is not off-hand statements of either meaning or its absence, but a thorough consideration of the problem of the migration of symbols, as Goblet d'Alviella called it, and the construction of a methodology for the interpretation of those art forms which recur in time and place, move from one religion to another. So only can we approach agreement upon the matter of whether a given form is "decorative" or "symbolic," as well as agreement upon what we mean by symbolic, and upon a method for evaluating symbolic content when present.

My problem specifically is so to study the Jewish art that it could be made into reliable and accepted historical evidence for the type of Judaism which produced it. This is the task which I am trying to work out in the study I have mentioned.

The first volume of my study had obviously to be given to collecting and presenting the Jewish art itself. One of my colleagues, after I had given a lecture with slides, in which I had shown a little of it, remarked with a sign that he wished this material was easier on the eyes. It is indeed for the most part very poor art, and beautifully as the Bollingen Foundation is reproducing it, nothing can make the drawings and carvings themselves beautiful. From the point of the history of symbolism, however, this is not a drawback. It is hard to consider that much of the wall painting in Pompeii is symbolic, for example, just because it is so well done, so ornamental, that it seems often irrelevant to ask whether it is also symbolic. That difficulty does not bother us in the Jewish material. Much of it, scratched hideously by amateurs in graves, could obviously never have been thought to be ornamental by any human being: its very crudity shows that it was put on the graves for something else besides decoration, a something else which would seem at once to be its symbolic value. The paintings of the Dura synagogue are conspicuously absent from this first volume for several reasons. First they, as O.T. illustration, present an entirely different problem from the other Jewish art. Secondly Volume I was quite large enough without them. Thirdly the right of prior publication of the pictures from Dura was officially assigned to my colleague Carl Kraeling, now at Chicago, and he has naturally been reluctant to let me publish before him the best of his photographs, though he has been most kind to let me study them freely as I wished. His volume on the Dura Synagogue, planned, I believe, on quite the conventional lines of art and archeological report, will be published in a year or so, I trust. So my consideration of the art of Dura, except for its pagan elements, must wait for Volume V of my study [in fact: vols. IX-XI (eds.)].

Meanwhile, never forgetting that the O.T. art of Dura is in the offing, it really clarifies the problem to attack by itself the question of "syncretism" as presented in the other Jewish representations. So in Volume II this problem of method of interpreting symbols which recur in different periods, places, and religions is directly attacked, and it is a resume of one of those chapters that I read to you here.

First it must be assumed in our methodology that we must use to the full the older methodology, which would explain art out of what literary remains exist to go with it. The natural thing, the inevitable thing, for example, is to explain Egyptian art, at least in the first instance, in terms of what we get from Egyptian literature and inscriptions. This method has its limitations, when we tend to assume that what is not explained in the literature is purely "ornamental," without any importance; that is, tend to treat the artistic symbol as essentially secondary to the literary evidence, and tend to forget that the men who wrote the books rarely carved the statues, or the devices on the graves. Valuable as literary evidence is when we can get it, however, in the case of the Jewish art I am studying this approach entirely breaks down, for we have not a line of ancient Jewish literature which seems to me directly relevant in the sense that it came from the Jews who made this art. To say that the art is Jewish and that the Talmud and older Midrash were being written by Jews in the same period, and hence that the art must be explained in terms of ideas in the Talmud and Midrash seems to me entirely fallacious. For everything goes to show that while occasionally a rabbi can be found who expressed some tolerance of this art, "did not forbid it" is the phrase, in general the rabbis have been correctly interpreted ever since by Jewish orthodoxy as discouraging, if not forbidding, any pictorial representation whatever. The meaning of the art, if it has any, will be found in the minds of those who took the initiative in making it, or having it made, not in the opinions of people interested in quite other things, some of whom tolerated it. Of such initiative there is not the slightest trace in rabbinic tradition, and we must naturally ascribe its origin to a non-rabbinic, popular Judaism. When we recall that this art developed largely among Greek-speaking Jews even in Palestine, as the inscriptions tell us; and that the Talmud, not completed until 400 A.D., was never translated like the Torah into either Greek or Latin in ancient times, we see that there is no reason whatever to suppose that the Jews who made this shocking art, shocking, that is, from the point of view of rabbinic orthodoxy, were activated or limited by rabbinic points of view in their art or in their thinking.

The Jewish art becomes then, what Cumont called his Mithraic material, a "picture book without texts." Philological approach to it has to be discarded. Obviously, when discussing such a symbol as the cup, for example, every reference to the drinking of wine which we can get from Jewish literature, including that of the rabbis, will have to be closely scrutinized; but we cannot begin by assuming that the rabbis have told us all that we can believe was in the minds of Jews who put the cup, or grapes, between peacocks in their synagogues, or who put the cup on their graves. The symbols, the art, that is, must be treated as primary evidence, not simply of art, but of the life of the Jews who made it. To use such evidence we must learn to read the symbols as such, and here we are on ground which the historian properly regards as extremely dangerous, the quicksand of scholarship which engulfs, often maddens, those who attempt to explore it. It is clear that we cannot just sit back and make guesses at meanings, or absence of meanings – there must be some sounder approach.

In trying thus to construct a methodology for discussing symbolism there is no escaping the problems of psychology. Without attempting to say what is my precise debt to various schools of philosophy or psychology, I may say that I have found the language of Suzanne Langer very congenial, especially in her distinguishing between the realms of denotative and of connotative thinking. Indeed this sort of distinction is being independently used not only by psychologists and philosophers, but by literary and art critics in America. It is a distinction largely between verbal and averbal thought, though this must quickly be modified since the connotative element is very important in language also. We think, that is, on two levels, one in which language is precise, scientific, specific, and attempts to convey a single definite idea from one mind to others. Such I am trying to do as I write: *préciser* the French actually call it. It is extremely difficult to do. I can describe external incidents, a walk to the village, because we have the language for such narration. The formulas of chemistry and mathematics are even more precise forms of expression than ordinary words. But behind this precision is our ordinary thought world where thinking is by no means precise, where our thoughts are occupied with impressions, associations, in words, tone of voice, forms of objects, of some of which we are aware, of much of which we are not aware ordinarily at all, and much of which is to be brought to awareness only by hypnotism, psychoanalysis, or the like. I have no interest in adapting this contrast in most of our thought with such categorising words as "pre-conscious," "sub-conscious," "unconscious." But I have enormous interest in the fact that all our most important thinking is in this world of the suggestive, connotative, meanings of words, objects, sounds, and forms; that our thinking is primarily unprecise; and that our world of precision is a veneer, a *tour de force*, which we superimpose upon our ordinary thought world of association. The present generation is amazingly developing both these types of thinking. At just the time when the vocabulary of science is becoming increasingly complex to try to achieve increasing precision, and when the great discoveries of science are made possible by such increased precision; modern poetry, art, music, find they can express the modern spirit only by abandoning the specific and formal and letting the unformed speak in ways quite maddening to those who still try to be verbally precise.

It is no accident that those who practise such "modern" art and writing use with natural sense of fitness the word "symbolism" when they are forced to *préciser* their lack of precision. By definition the symbol is a word, a poem, a musical sound, which means more to us than the literal word or thing itself. For example, the word apple when used specifically to designate a certain kind of fruit is a word of precision. It makes little difference whether we say *apple, apfel,* or *pomme.* The sounds are useful, not in themselves, but only as they suggest a specific sort of fruit. Similarly the drawing of an apple in a dictionary, or in a treatise on fruit trees, is only another way of making precise the concept which is being conveyed from one mind to another. But when the word apple, in any language, refers to the apple awarded by Paris, or to the apple eaten by Adam, then the form of the apple, even whether it was an apple at all, is unimportant – for the word has become a symbol for greed, jealousy, discord, in one case, for disobedience to God, sin, in another. If I say, "The lady offered him her apple, and, as from the days of Adam, he took and ate," I am not talking about apples at all, but about woman's sexual appeal for man. It would indeed be difficult to *préciser* all that the word apple meant in that sentence. For some it would mean the acceptably desired; for some it is still the quintessence of sin; for most of us it is both at the same time with associations that go far down into our unknown depths and conflicts.

If this statement had been made in a poem, or in some other form of "creative" writing, the author would think that a Professor who tried to make its meanings explicit and denotative was a pedantic fool. The Professor would probably think he was being intellectual, superior, in trying to do so. The cleft between the literary, poetic mind, and the academic mind is largely the cleft between the mind which expresses itself, lives directly and deeply, in symbolic meanings, and the mind which supposes this sort of thought improved by annotated editions. It is the cleft between what I am calling "meaning" on the one hand and "explanations" on the other. The symbol carries its own meaning, and with it its own power to move us. The explanation is for some people indispensable, but it is never the thing, the thought of our poet, itself.

This sort of distinction is most helpful for the understanding of creation in art, music, and the rest, where the symbols of chiaroscuro, of color, or of form, or the symbol of successions of melodies, harmonies and discords, become the immediate vehicles of meaning, vehicles which eternally deride every attempt to make their meaning verbally precise. The old distinction between the emotional and the intellectual here breaks down completely, for we see that the deepest thought and meaning is in the world of symbol. Explanations are always a weak afterthought as compared to meaning itself. And significant meaning is almost always conveyed in symbols, in which I should include now drama, myth, ritual, all connotative meanings of words, as well as distinctive forms. This is the real function of dreams as conceived by the depth psychologists: they are a procession of symbols, symbolic not only in their forms, but in what happens to the forms in the action of the dream. When we become psychologically disturbed we must have help to make these deeper symbols of ours verbal, give them explanations. Dr. Jung has said the same of his "archetypes" when he says that the symbol itself is neither the literal sun, nor the lion or king for which it is a symbol, but an "unknown third thing that finds expression in all these similes, yet – to the perpetual vexation of the intellect – remains unknown and not to be fitted into a formula."[1] Ordinarily, however, the dream is nature's own psychiatry: a sign not that we are in psychological difficulties but that we are getting dramatic purgation as the conflicts and disturbed elements within us express themselves in the medium of dream-symbolism.

My interest in all this was to come closer to an understanding of religious symbols. It now appears that we have gone a long way toward making clear to ourselves what we mean, in "precise" terms, by the word symbol. As in general, it was a word or form which expressed more than it indicated, now we see that in religion we must add that the symbol is not only a direct purveyor of meaning in itself, but also a thing of power, one which operates upon us to inspire, to release tensions, to arouse guilt, or to bring a sense of forgiveness and reconciliation. We can love the symbol, we can hate it, but so long as it is a symbol we register its message, feel its power. A most moving story was told me by a famous early refugee from Hitlerian Germany, who, when the full meaning of Nazism was presented to him at a meeting, when he grasped what was in the swastika and behind it, stood in the street after the meeting shaking his fist at the great swastika on the building and shouting at the top of his voice, "It's a damnable thing, a damnable symbol." His friends almost violently took

---

[1] C.G. Jung and C. Kerényi, *Introduction to a Science of Mythology*, 1951, 105; cf. pp. 127, 136, and the quotation from Schelling by Kerényi, p. 214.

him home, and got him out of the country. He has been convinced ever since that some symbols are in their very form good, some evil. My point in recalling his adventure is simply to emphasize that a symbol in religion (and here my definition of religion would include the swastika with the cross as both powerful religious symbols) is something which conveys meaning, yes, but which also has inherent power to operate upon us. Indeed our lives are largely guided and moulded by symbols. There are the symbolic acts of polite society, the "code" of a gentlemen which no one could codify without becoming ridiculous: the urges and repressions of phallicism, so powerful a symbol that in our civilization we can rarely contemplate it directly at all; the symbolic force of green to the Irishman, of red to the communist; such symbolic words as husband, wife, mother, father, child; the public symbols of the flag, the shield of David, the Cross; and there is the world of private symbolism manifest in our dreams and neurotic compulsions.

It would be relatively easy if on this basis we could get in words a common formula of meaning for each symbol, at least for the public symbols, and suppose that meaning, or operative power, was always conveyed by that symbol whenever it appeared. But this is to miss the point with which we began, that symbols have a way of dying, or apparently losing their power, and becoming merely ornaments. And they also have the power of coming to life again, as fresh associations and religious awakenings take one of the old symbols for their own. This happened when the Christians adopted the old, the universal symbol of the cross, a symbol which in pre-Christian ornament had degenerated to be only the four pointed rosette, one of many forms of the rosette. The rosettes were still actively symbolic when Christianity was born, continued to be so late into Byzantine Christianity, but the four-point rosette, in a circle, or abbreviated as the swastika, had come in the pagan world to have no special significance that I can see in itself, though the swastika form can make a better case for itself than the simple four-point rosette in a circle. Christianity seized upon this four-point rosette in a circle, however, then still later made it specifically Christian by using the longer upright shaft, and thus took it out of the circle, although the Coptic Church and the Eastern Church preferred to let it stay there. Similarly the sudden revival from the dead, or nearly dead, which recently occurred to the swastika was even more dramatic. Now it would be silly to argue that Christians put nothing new into the cross; or that Hitler's swastika meant the same as the swastika on a Greco-Roman mummy, or on a Jewish tombstone from the ancient world. But it is significant that if a new movement wants a powerful symbol, it usually finds satisfaction in reviving one of the primordial symbols rather than in inventing new ones, and the presumption is that it does so because there is inherent symbolic power of some kind at least dormant in the old symbols even when we suppose that they have become "purely decorative." Whether there is such dormant symbolic power in what may ordinarily be called dead symbols used for ornament, it is not for the historian to debate. He must leave this for further investigation by psychologists. Whether it is correct to talk about basic symbols which *die,* or which merely become quiescent, I cannot say. Yet the trouble is that one cannot leave the question without begging it. For we must continue to face the problem of the "merely decorative" as contrasted with the "symbolic" use of forms in art; and when we contrast them in these terms, or in such terms as "live" symbols versus "dead" symbols, or of "active" symbols versus "quiescent" or "dormant" symbols in each case, we assume a theory of the nature of the contrast. Since I must have a terminology, I shall arbitrarily, tentatively, and without prejudice, use the contrast "live" and "dead," fully prepared to have that terminology corrected by better knowledge.

For in my work I cannot wait for this problem to be solved. As an historian I see that there is a great contrast between what is involved in the transition of what I call a "live" symbol from one religion to another in contrast to the transition of "dead" symbols. The difference can perhaps best be indicated by illustration. If in a modern Jewish synagogue, where ornament is increasingly being used, one should find a large cross on the Torah shrine, it would be obvious that though the group still wanted to call themselves Jews (the living symbol of the synagogue and Torah shrine would indicate this) they had openly taken some highly important Christian values into their Judaism. One would need no literary documents to prove this. The presence of the "live" Christian symbol, the cross, would in itself indicate this at once. If one could get written explanations of the phenomenon from the rabbi of the synagogue, that would be only supplementary, perhaps quite sophistic, rationalization. The explanations would obviously be of less importance than the *value,* the direct operative power, of the cross itself to carry Christian types of experience in religion into the lives of the Jews in that hypothetical synagogue.

From such a hypothetical, probably impossible, case we turn to actual cases all over the world when the Catholic church (rarely the Protestant) has allowed converted natives to carry much of their older symbolism into the new Catholic chapels. The phenomenon is most familiar in the Latin-American countries of America, where native forms, symbols, and even elaborate rites, are kept up along with the Christian ones, often right in the Christian churches. The Catholic clergy is quite aware that this gives to the native Christianity a different coloration from the Catholicism of Italy or Ireland. So long as the symbols or rites carried over are "live," actively operative, they cannot be carried over without bringing into the new religion the older "values." Explanations must then be given, as when, in a story F.C. Conybeare liked to tell, a Jesuit priest had got a community in one of the Pacific Islands to call "Francis of Assisi" a native statue which they insisted on having at least in the narthex of the chapel. Calling the figure Francis of Assisi did soften the paganism of the figure a bit, but did more to ameliorate the conscience of the priest who allowed it than to put the values of the Italian Saint into the savage figure. That figure for the natives, we may be sure, kept its original living values in spite of the ridiculous "explanation" taught them by the priest.

The migration of symbols in the ancient world followed, I am sure, the same lines. The egg and dart molding may have originally had symbolic value, but it had become quite a conventional ornament long before the beginning of the Christian era, and its appropriation by Jews and Christians probably meant nothing more than that this sort of design for a moulding pleased them. The zig-zag line, so much used in romanesque architecture, is less certainly a case of the purely formal, for it is the primordial symbol of water, and even in romanesque ornament was used over doorways of churches in a way to suggest that the divine flow of grace, which water meant in antiquity, was still being felt by those who entered under it to worship in the churches. Even more clearly alive are the symbols I am studying, the eagle, the lion, the fish, the Winged Victory and the wreath, the caduceus of Hermes, the figure of Orpheus and the animals. The persistence of these in Jewish and Christian art cannot be presumed to be the persistence of the merely ornamental, the dead, for these were living symbols in paganism, and as we know they remained living symbols in Christianity, so that presumably, to my mind inevitably, they were living symbols to the Jews. Stripped of their old pagan explanations, as the Jesuit stripped the name and mythology from the savage figure when he called it Francis of Assisi, still these could have been retained by Christians, and Jews, only because there was a value in them which they wanted to preserve for themselves. If Orpheus later became a symbol of Christ taming the passions for Christians, he probably had been Moses or David, or some other Jewish figure doing this for Jews when drawn in a Jewish synagogue. Indeed when the religious symbols borrowed by Jews in these years were put together, it became clear that the material borrowed was not merely a "picture-book without text," but itself a *lingua franca* taken into most of the religions of the day. It was a symbolic language, a direct language of values, however, not a language of the denotative mind. Orpheus could become Christ because he had ceased to be specifically Orpheus before the Christians borrowed him, and had come to represent the mastery of the passions by the spirit without specific name or mythology. Helios driving his chariot through the zodiac could be used by Jews to represent their cosmic deity because in the thinking of the day, especially the sort of thinking associated with Neoplatonism, this symbol had come to stand not for a specific anthropomorphic God at all, but for the supreme principle to be borrowed and used by all sorts of religions at the time. So its presence to our knowledge on the floors of three synagogues in Palestine indicates that Jews had in their Judaism not *Helios,* the pagan god, but the value of that figure in contemporary life.

To understand the Judaism which used these pagan symbols, then, it is necessary to reconstruct the *lingua franca* of this symbolism, as it was used for Osiris, Mithras, Dionysos, Sabazius, Attis, and Christianity. To do this requires the investigation of the use of each of the symbols in as many as possible of the religions which used them, even back to the earliest use in Mesopotamia and Egypt when they can be traced that far. If continuity of symbolic value can be demonstrated in all these religions, this would establish a meaning of the *lingua franca* which, as it seems to have stability for other religions, would increasingly suggest itself as the meaning of the symbols also for Jews. In all this, however, we have constantly to bear in mind that the "meaning" will not be a "denotative," "precise," "explanatory" meaning, but a connotative one, a meaning in a language which spoke to the mind verbally unformed, which has more immediate relation to the emotions than has our verbal mind. More than simply arouse emotions, however, these symbols would carry an emotionally potent idea, even though the names or the myths for a given symbol might change indefinitely in the verbal formulations of the various cults. The reconstruction is one which will hardly please the modern philologist, who will expect me to say in precise *words* what Helios meant, or Orpheus, or the Winged Victory, or the eagle. This, let me repeat, is like expecting me to put a modern symbolistic poem into discoursive prose, though even more difficult. People used symbols which could pass thus from religion to religion precisely because the symbols did not have any precise, denotative, meaning, but spoke to a level of consciousness or mentality much less precise, but much richer and more important than the level of precise denotation. Christianity and Judaism would unite in rejecting Dionysos and his rites and myths with horror, while they kept his symbols. They rejected the specific and kept what I may call the sub-specific – linguistically, that is. There is a meaning to the symbol, however, which is grasped by the devout quite as directly as verbal language, in the great majority of cases far more directly. That our explanations of why the cross is important would so widely conflict, cannot obscure the fact that actually the cross itself in its own way carries a much more concrete and definite meaning than all the verbal explanations of it put together. Theology is for the few: the cross is for all, intellectual and stupid alike. It is this language which the historian of symbols must come to understand: he must let the *lingua franca* speak to him as directly as Bach speaks in his fugues to those who know Bach's language. The importance of Dura now emerges: here is the confluence of pictorial symbol with philological text, since the scene represents, however fancifully, O.T. incidents. Dura gives us a key to the sort of Jewish explanations, theory, use of texts, of Jewish tradition, which went with the borrowed pagan art. One can of course look at these paintings, identify the scenes and make guesses at their meaning, but that would give as little help for real understanding as have all the discussions of the pictures I have yet seen. It is the great mass of symbolic evidence which first gives us a clue to the meanings in the deeper sense which these O.T. pictures were designed to naturalize in Jewish terms.

To take a single example: In one narrative painting at Dura two incidents are presented. In the first incident a naked slave girl in the reedy water holds high the baby Moses whom she has just taken from the little ark of bulrushes beside her. At the left stand two women, one of these again with the child. These women have been variously interpreted. Apparently they are either bringing Moses to be put into the ark, or they represent his acceptance by the Princess who gives him to Miriam to take to his mother for nursing. Perhaps the women suggest both events, and their symbolism is none the worse for doing so. At the right of the painting is another scene where Pharaoh, with the usual two throne-guards, apparently accepts the child. The same two women stand before him, and the slave girl, now clothed, crouches over an object, presumably the baby Moses, which has been lost with the destruction of the lower part of this section of the painting. So far all is relatively straight-forward and literal: there is no symbolic interpretation. But in the center, just above the baby Moses as the slave girl holds him high above her, stand the proverbial three nymphs, one with the usual shell, another with the shell and pitcher, and the central one with a box which recalls the boxes often in the hands of the Magi as they come to the infant Jesus in Christian paintings. The three nymphs are thus with the baby carrying their standard symbols of potency, the shell and the pitcher, but bringing this baby special gifts of some sort. When now we recall the value of the figures of the nymphs, we are deep in symbolic interpretation indeed. For the nymphs were the nurses of divine babies, babies who were actual gods, or were heroes with divine powers. Their shells are symbols of this divine nativity: a mosaic I recently saw in Beirut, for example, soon to be published, shows a nymph, so labelled in the mosaic, beside "Alexander" who is a small child being born, rising out of a shell. This mosaic must have been roughly contemporary with the Dura scene. The nymphs with their shell, then, are a living symbol introduced into this scene where Moses is finally accepted by Pharaoh, and would seem plainly to indicate that the Jews of Dura considered Moses more than an ordinary human being, the divine baby, just as the makers of the Beirut mosaic certainly were representing that "Alexander" was more than an ordinary human being. The fact that such an interpretation would go much further than rabbinic and later orthodox Judaism would care to push the dignity of Moses has nothing to do with the patent fact that Moses was actually painted there with the nymphs, and that it is inconceivable that such a group should have been taken from pagan scenes of infancy and put so neatly in a scene of the infancy of Moses without a continuity of the value of those nymphs, and hence a declaration of at least the quasi-divinity of Moses himself. The Jews who made this declaration were probably quite as indifferent, indeed hostile, to the myths about nymphs as were Christians who painted Orpheus as Christ to the myths of Orpheus. To regard the Dura painting as in any primary sense a picture of nymphs, or the invasion into Judaism as nuymphs as such, would seem to be a complete misunderstanding. So Orpheus as a person never invaded Christianity or Judaism. What is represented is a picture of the super-human character of Moses, with nymphs used simply as a convention to represent that character in the infant Moses. The nymphs are not "simply conventional," however, any more than a word with meaning is simply conventional. The way of conveying the idea of super-human children was to put nymphs with their shells and gifts beside him. The nymphs are a word in the *lingua franca,* that is they convey a definite idea: not so definite as we should like for we do not know whether they show that Moses in the painting was super-human as Alexander was super-human or as Apollo, also nursed by nymphs, was super-human. But even the words of philologians often leave many problems of precision. We must see, however, that in the language of values, the nymphs have told us a great deal about the Judaism of the Jews in Dura.

This was a simple and obvious case; unfortunately we have not many such simple cases. The white Greek robe worn by all the chief characters in the Dura paintings is precisely the robe worn by the followers of Isis and Osiris in most of the mummy portraits from Hellenistic and Roman Egypt. It later became the uniform of sanctity and sainthood for Christian saints in the first six centuries of Christian art. Presumably it marks the outstanding sanctity of the great Jews who wear it in the paintings also, and probably carries over many of the connotations of sanctity in the sense common to followers of Osiris and Christ, especially the prerogative of immortality and the power to help others into immortality.

Much more complicated than the task of applying such symbolic meanings to the Dura scenes (which must now be supplemented, of course, by scenes from the early Christian paintings descendant from such Jewish art) is the recovery of the basic Jewish meaning of the *lingua franca* of the purely pagan symbols themselves.

I have said that this meaning is to be recovered only by carefully tracing each of the symbols through all the civilizations and religions in the ancient world which used them. Anything contemporary in writing referring to such symbols would be, of course, of the greatest value, but such references are so sporadic that we must draw most of our conclusions without the help of any literary references whatever. What I do in this particular I do as a historian, and the re-emergence of the same basic symbols in dreams and hallucinations, whose importance Dr. Jung has so properly stressed, or in various parts of the world as anthropologists so well know, will all be most relevant to final understanding. My pedestrian job as a historian is to study the *lingua franca* in historical, temporal contiguity, from paganism, through Judaism, into Christianity.

So excusing me from responsibility for considering the religious aspirations of Brahmins, Confucianists, Fiji Islanders, or American Indians, or the religious drives of modern neurotics, you may be interested in a general summary (here it must be completely without demonstration) of what the transition of those symbols seems to me to indicate for the religious aspirations of the people who used the symbols. But to do this I must go into another excursus to explain briefly the psychological premises on which my historical evaluations are based.

It seems to me that the symbols deeply express a basic longing of man for life. This is by no means a novel major premise: the "instinct of self-preservation" is as familiar from the older psychologies as the "life-urge" in the newer. We recall Dr. Jung's phase: "The strongest, the most ineluctable urge in every being, namely the urge to realize itself."[2] Everything indicates that this was a very unreflective urge with primitive man, as it is with animals. Savages and animals will alike fight to the death for their food, just as periodically they will fight to the death for the desired female. But the desire for the female certainly plays little part in the conscious motivation of most animals (except when they are periodically inflamed by her odor), while they spend the majority of their waking hours in search for food. Yet the life urge seems intimately to include the sex urge, increasingly so as man becomes more civilized, the sex urge not only in the relatively sophisticated desire for progeny, but in the desire for the personal enlargement and achievement, expression and experience of life, which the sexual act itself brings with it.

The sex urge, accordingly, I must take as but one aspect of the profound urge to life, to its realization, expansion, and perpetuation. In this, so far as I understand them, I agree with both Freud and Jung who alike insist that their "libido" includes much more than the sex urge. With the view of sex itself as the door to something greater one must not confuse the "sublimations" and "perversions" of the sex impulse which for one reason or another may take the place of direct expression of the instinct through the sexual act. Indeed I am not sure that to say that artistic creation is a case of sublimation of sexual activity is at all correct: any more than one can say that because water flows more strongly through one tap if a second tap on the same main is shut off, the greater flow of the first tap is a sublimation of the flow of the second. The one tap is simply getting more from the flow behind both. Sexual activity occurs only when one's great stream of life-urge expresses itself through one's sexual mechanism (which is much more than the sexual organs). When the life stream is shut off from sexual expression it may find other outlets, but is then very debatedly to be called in any sense sexual activity. So I prefer to speak of the life-urge, rather than "libido," since the specific sexual connotations of the word "libido" have caused so much confusion.

While the most immediate external satisfaction of the life-urge is in eating and sex (and of course breathing, which we take for granted), with them go the primitive outlets of warfare and the hunt, the urge to kill, familiar, unfortunately, still. Killing is now episodic in its literal form, but a substitute outlet had to be found in sport and social-economic competition. The great symbols of the life-urge are by nature of three basic kinds, those of hunting, killing or fighting; those of food and eating (or of the sources of food, the winds, rain, sun, etc.); and those of sex. These symbols are rarely presented completely distinct from one another; though a given symbol will be basically one of them, it will almost certainly contain at least two of the three elements. With these three we have the vast majority of religious symbols used by any but the most advanced and abstract peoples.

---

[2]*Op. cit.*, p. 124.

Another source of religious symbolism is much more subjective or personal than these; it springs from the child's relation with his parents in infancy. The life of the little baby fifty thousand years ago was far more like our experiences at the same age than any of his subsequent experiences. And it is the unchangeable nature of these experiences which furnishes one of the most important common grounds of understanding between us and remote civilizations.

The baby has always had, if he survived at all, a passionate life-urge, and very little else. To be sure healthy infants express this life-urge the greater part of the time in sleep, a way of life through death. Their waking moments are taken up with a sense of great discomfort from their hunger, thirst, and elimination, and with the ecstasy of the gratification of these desires. The baby awakens with that terrifying confusion which is sometimes upon us adults when we awaken. Their world is only a few feet, at first only a few inches, in circumference, their misery, helplessness, and terrors are their only conscious experience. They cry – and out of the mystery suddenly appears a loving face and deft hands which cut the terrible aloneness and promise the satisfaction of all needs. Soon the infant is comfortable, and then comes the heavenly breast, where love, and food, and life are one. Insecurity, fear, uncertainty, are lost in perfect peace and trust. Satisfied with a divine completeness and security the infant sucks in the life of the great goddess, and perhaps gurgles in brief joy before it again takes the sleepy path of death to still greater life. No later type of experience ever equals the complete satisfaction of this. In maturity an ideal love affair may reproduce some of it, but only in societies of romantic love-patterns could such perfection last for more than fleeting moments. In no adult relation is the experience at all complete.

The pang of later infancy is the invasion of this ideal world by social realities and compulsions which spoil one after the other the perfection of early gratifications. Defecation, from a pure delight, becomes to the child a subject of meaningless struggle; when bodily movements begin, the loving face of the goddess often grows stern as it imposes incomprehensible restrictions and prohibitions, and then the breast itself is lost. Indeed even monotheism becomes a confusing polytheism as the goddess, still supreme, takes her place among other great figures which appear and disappear like theophanies. A world has passed away, one where in love a goddess's own person gave full gratification of the life-urge. Specific memories of these months mercifully fade away, and do not haunt us, but the basic memory does remain as the one time when life completely conquered death in love. The nostalgia of later years, in terms of more mature concepts, is still for those arms, everlasting arms in which we can find again our mother's warmth and life, keep it now at last forever, if it is not for the complete Nirvana of the womb.

Each aspect of this experience and its deprivation has appeared as a major cause of later psychological difficulty. But I do not think that for religion the experience as a whole, first of gratification and then of deprivation, has been sufficiently stressed; it is the basis of at least one of the most important of the patterns of religion. This pattern of religion produces little "social gospel": It is as narcissistic as the life of the infant. It is the craving of the individual for absorption in the true Being, for life after death, for forgiveness and reconciliation, for rebirth and the abiding presence of the Comforter. The "mystic marriage," in the form of union with the temple prostitute or with the Church which is the bride of Christ, is really a union with the Great Mother, a return to her intimate care. We love the picture of the Christian version of this, Mary the Mother of her Child, for we are the child. We project ourselves into the picture, but never as Mary – always we, at least we males, are the baby in her arms. And the power that Baby manifests is the power we want also to manifest, an overflow of life such as we feel we should have in the security of that embrace. Ave, Maria! Yes indeed we pray for her loving protection, whether before a figure of the Mother, or in primitive sexual rites, or in the scarcely veiled eroticism of Protestant hymnody.

As the child goes into the next stage of his development the love and protection of the great beings of the adult world are still of intense importance. But the life of law and taboo is now the much more immediate concern of the child's consciousness. Still it is the life and protection, the flow of loving approval, which the child so desperately wants, but he finds that it is now to be bought at a price: it no longer flows to him freely. The mother goddess has by now become a male-female duality, or monad in two persons, father and mother, and the child soon learns (in the normal family of the millennia of our own civilization) that the ultimate authority is not the mother but the father. "I'll tell your father" is the final threat in the child's life. The law he must obey is to him really a codification of the whims and fancies of his father. The sanction is the father-mother displeasure, or even the hell-tortures of whipping. From this one can never feel safe except in the atmosphere of approval and love which only obedience seems to produce. The "super-ego" is rapidly forming at this time: God and my father are one, and *Ave Maria, ora pro me,* intercede for me with the Father, is the instinctive, inevitable, attitude toward the mother. At this level again the religion of many is found. To the original pure nostalgia for complete gratification has been added a sense that the price of gratification is obedience to laws, social and ritualistic, while the concept of the mediator has made its highly important appearance.

The fully "compulsory" stage of Freudianism is a step beyond this, but not away from it. Law becomes more elaborate, mediation less important, and a religion can emerge, like talmudic Judaism, where the mother element has become quite unrecognizably obscured in the dominant pattern of the direct relation between a boy and his father. One is here given the rewards of this life and the next strictly on the basis of obedience. To be sure the quality of mercy has not failed, and provision is made for repentance and reinstatement of the transgressor. But these never were so important in Judaism that they produced a distinct divine personality to symbolize and execute them. Traditional Judaism is a civilization, a whole way of life, but only secondarily a personal source of ecstasy. It is intensely social in feeling, as the family is a social unit, where the children know that the father is equally concerned with the brothers and sisters. Little of social importance came out of the cult of the Virgin, or of the Great Mother or of Isis. The social aspects of religion first became important with the importance of the father, and the tendency came to its logical end when it produced a sense of the Father-God's universal rightness, and of universal Right. Such a religion gets its hold upon its followers through the conditioning power of behavior. The family festival comes to play a tremendous part in the child's life, so that, like Christmas for Christians, however far a Jew may go from orthodox Jewish belief, he rarely ceases to feel an appeal in the Festivals if he was brought up in them. This gripping hold of Jewish observances is magnificently presented in Feuchtwanger's *Jud Süß*. Behaviour, repetition, can of course instill a much more ecstatic and personal religious pattern than is usually associated with the Jewish festivals. In a religious pattern such as that of rabbinic Judaism, however, observance chiefly enforces, binds the believers to the compulsory pattern of life with the Father.

Religious experiences can thus be divided quite sharply between the infantile narcissistic mother pattern and the later compulsory pattern of legalism. To be sure the great religions have for the most part contained both elements. Certainly Christianity, with its Old Testament, and the ethical teachings of Jesus, has not been, at any time, engrossed simply in the problem of personal salvation. On the contrary, even Judaism, commentators are now agreed, drew as heavily for its spirit upon the fertility religions of the Canaanites as upon the distinctive "religion of Moses." Most of Jewish rituals and festivals go back to fertility rites. Still there can be no doubt that the Jewish contribution to Christianity through the Old Testament and the teaching of the Synoptics was that of a relation between a Father and his children, while the Greek contribution of Paul, the Fourth Gospel, and the early Greek Christians was in the direction of a personal religion of salvation that in emotional pattern resembled much more the ancient fertility cults than the teachings of the Rabbis.

Regarded from the point of view of such a contrast in religious types, that is between the mystical and the legalistic types, the Jewish archeological material became increasingly anomalous as I studied its associations elsewhere. The symbols borrowed from pagan art by the Jews were precisely those symbols which stood for the type of religious experience and longing most completely in contrast with tendencies of rabbinic Judaism in the same centuries. That is, the rabbis were developing Judaism increasingly for its legalism, its "compulsory" pattern. The victory of Yahwism over the Canaanites was at last coming to completion. Fertility rites, the cycle of Adonis dead and risen, the birth of the sacred child at the spring time and at the winter solstice, the holy trinity of

Father, Mother, Son, in which the son was identical with the Father, all these were being finally expelled from Judaism, even in the Hosean form. God was a loving Father, but intensely masculine, and the task of his children was to study his Law. Nothing in this led, or could have led, anyone to suspect that in the very centuries when the Rabbis, in their scholastic groups in Jamnia and Babylon, were patiently working out the Talmud, with its almost exclusively legal interest, in just those centuries the Jews had broken down the traditional restrictions and covered their synagogues and graves with symbols partly Jewish and partly from that paganism which was especially hateful to the Rabbis. In Christianity these same symbols were being used to represent again just those aspects of the new faith most repugnant to the rabbinic schools. Nothing whatever warrants either our saying that the symbols had no meaning in Judaism, or our insistence that somehow if they had meaning that meaning must be found in rabbinic thinking. That is nothing warrants such treatment of this material but the traditions of philology, which cling to the written records, and hate to adopt ideas of the past from anything but verbal statements.

We have suggested that the *lingua franca* of symbolism, or the continuity of values, was the key to understanding the Jewish symbols, and that the *lingua franca* could be read, the values could be recovered, only as we saw the problem of figured symbolism in the light of the newer psychology. And we have suggested that with the psychological understanding we must follow each symbol through all of its typical appearances in those countries and ages whose influence carried on, directly or indirectly, into the Greco-Roman world. The elements of a psychology of religion just suggested were the product of this search, not its guide. That psychology of religion, I have said, centers in a great life-urge, a drive to security which may express itself in desire for mystic union with the Mother, or for security by obedience to the Father. But the symbols, as I studied them first, amazed me by seeming to reduce themselves in almost every case to a basic erotic value. As I took up each symbol I hoped I should at last get something different. But when even the dove, duck, and the quail were by specific ancient testimony given erotic explanations I felt myself overcome by the evidence itself. To the investigator this experience is much more moving than it can ever be to the mere reader. Only by taking my book apart and looking up these could the experience of the author be duplicated, his experience, that is, where as he took up symbol after symbol, he found himself driven into the same sort of explanations, the same basic values, for each with relentless regularity, driven not by his own predilections, but by the evidence itself.

The basic value, I have said, was definitely erotic. This was the major element all the symbols had in common. How could this happen when religious eroticism had been so driven out of Judaism? It was partly in view of this that I looked with fresh eyes at the erotic element in religion in general. Was it eroticism in the sense that we use the term – namely something akin to the *ars amatoria,* a means of expressing or intensifying the pleasure of intercourse? It suddenly occurred to me that to evaluate a leather phallus in Greek society it was necessary to think of it *in Greek society*, not to project our still half Victorian conceptions back upon it, or to think how inappropriate a phallus would be in a Protestant chapel. Whether you and I think the phallus a proper symbol for deity has nothing whatever to do with the patent fact that the Greek, the Syrian, the Phoenician, and the Egyptian – with hosts of others – thought it was the best symbol of all. Whatever you and I think about sexual intercourse and its place in society, many ancient peoples regarded it for millennia as one of the best forms of temple worship. Whether you and I have been accustomed to be amused at sexual humour, the peoples of the ancient world loved it and used it as part of their divine festivals. Though I rigorously refused to interpret pillars, upright stones, altars, etc., as phallic, after the manner of many historians of phallicism (though I am far from denying the possibility of their ultimate phallic value) I still was driven by the material associations in which the symbols I was investigating were used by Greeks, Egyptians, and many others to recognize in these a basic phallic meaning.

Again, what was that phallic meaning? In our day of repressed sex, phallic symbols in dreams and gestures are usually taken correctly to come from repressed desires for a sexual experience. But to carry this over to sexual symbols in an age with little such repression, and to suppose that a phallus was used by ancient worshippers similarly to symbolize literal sexual desires not otherwise to be released, is utterly unjustifiable, equally so on the part of those who make such interpretation directly, and on the part of those who implicitly make the same judgment when they refuse to consider this type of material at all. In the earliest times of our cultural development, when, as in Greece and Egypt, the symbol was most frankly used, there was little indication of sexual repression in society in our sense. Even the almost universal taboos against incest seem little known in Egypt. Nor was there an indication that religion was using the symbols as a brothel might use them in Pompeii, to enhance sexual titillation. Quite the reverse, everything indicates that the early devotee wanted from his phallic rites to be gratified with food, and with the perpetuation of his life. He used the symbols of gratification most nearly and naturally at hand in order to satisfy his desire. He used, that is, phallic symbols to represent his desire for food and life, because he had sex and did not always have enough food. Similarly in our society analysts tell me that the food we have is often in our dreams a symbol for the sexual experiences we think society keeps from us. We use what we have as symbols of gratification of desires for what we do not have. It was in fertility rites for his *crops* and *flocks* that the phallic symbol or rite seems most characteristically to appear, because crops and flocks represented food. The personal application of these symbols and rites, even their use for personal immortality, seems secondary to, and was probably historically later than, their use to get crops and flocks. It was the most obvious kind of sympathetic magic to make a field fertile by setting up a phallus in it, or by simulating or actually performing intercourse on it or for it. The utter frankness of the symbol in its early stages shows its completely different function and origin from any modern "nastiness." Men wanted crops and flocks, and used the phallus as a religious-magical symbol for its power to produce them. Not that they eliminated the element of pleasure from the symbol. Why should they? A bull is no less good as a general symbol of food because one likes beef. The sinfulness of sexual humor apparently had never occurred to them.

Once I came to recognize the complete naturalness of phallic symbolism as used in early times, its freedom from the moldiness of repressions, its "language" became clearer to me as I watched the history of the symbols. For as developing civilization began to distinguish between what it called the spiritual and fleshly, the good and the bad, the pure and the impure, the symbols lost their directness; the hideous silenus-satyr no longer raped maenads on the bases, or, ithyphallic, plucked and trampled the sacred grapes. Rather, satyrs became graceful young men with no symptom of lechery, and with only the pointed ears and merest suggestion of a tail to show their ancestry. As a competitor for their functions appeared the innocuous baby, the cupid, still a love symbol, and still performing the religious functions in the vine and elsewhere which the lascivious satyrs had earlier carried out. Then the cupids supplanted the satyrs altogether, and the satyrs survived only as devils in iconography, symbols now of the forbidden. The devil is still a Pan or a Satyr, primarily inviting us to sexuality. He is the devil because frank invitation to sexuality is taboo for us.

Suddenly it occurred to me that I had in my hands the historical antetype of the typical "psycho-analysis." Where analyses had over and again found that modern religion, especially of the ardent types, had at its roots sexual motivation, I was seeing through history an original body of frankly sexual symbols in religion disappear into indirections as society demanded their repression. The satyr had become a cupid, I repeat. But in their new and almost unrecognizable form the old drives kept their original central place in the new religions which more "civilized" cultures developed. Or to put it another way, a social analysis of the symbols of modern religion seemed to push back in history to the same sort of early association as is still to be found in the individual.

How did this come about? The religion of mysticism I have described in terms chiefly of the infant longing to find complete gratification of its life-urge in the person, the life substance, of the goddess. Yet quite as important, if not much more so, among the symbols of this experience are universally the symbols of sex. How do these come together, especially in view of the fact that I have distinguished sex as only one outlet for the life-urge?

This seems quite the most difficult problem of all in my nascent psychology of religion, and one that it is extremely dangerous to try to answer for any period but our own. Here anthropology might help indeed, in reconstructing what puberty means for the làd or girl in societies without restrictions, or at least without our restrictions, since I doubt that any contemporary society is without very definite sexual restrictions. Yet the fusion of the two motifs, sex and the Mother, whatever the mechanism, seems to me most natural. The lad's whole nature at puberty is stirred by new longings, the old drive to complete himself in some one else, but his new sexual potency now gives him a new means of accomplishing it. That it should recall the gratification of his babyhood seems again inevitable, as well as that the experience with a woman should, if only temporarily, identify itself with his earliest experiences with the mother. In adolescent years a boy is usually most moved by a woman older than himself, and even when in later years his craving is for the young girl, the virgin he can protect, and to whom he can play the ruling father, still the girl must often play the mother to him if he is to be happy with her. The religious other, the great mother, of whom he still dreams, becomes the virgin mother, I am sure, because in late years the mate desired is a virgin, and because the mother of religion is the immediate projection of the mother as freshly sought in a young virgin by the mature man. Denial to her of normal relation with the father while she still produces the son likewise enhances her value to the son. And in the highly complex picture of maturity the so called Oedipus complex gets its normal gratification, as the young man takes his father's role with the new little mother. Union is now naturally expressed in the symbols of sexual union. For the act of sex itself is usually most important because it gives a sense of life realization.

Hence in this mature quest for the mother, or for life in the mother, a quest which produced religions and mystical symbolism, the magico-religious symbols of the fertility cults, their sex-symbols, were the most natural at hand to develop and continue. Religion develops not by invention of new symbols but by putting new meanings into the old. There seem to have been three major steps in this development. At first the sex symbol was literal fertility magic to bring crops, as with a Priapus in a garden. Then man's sex experience as a door to the greater life for him came increasingly to be felt, and the sex symbols or acts could be used by identification as open means of achieving union with the deity, male or female. Finally all conscious reference to the sexual act would be eliminated, the overtly sexual pictures and rites would be abandoned, so that religion could achieve the "higher" gratification. Indeed in "higher" religions as in Plato's *Symposium* and the *Bacchae* of Euripides the sexual act is deplored or despised, a change which has created the amazing anomaly that the greatest single tension in all "higher" religions is precisely the tension between spirit and body, sex as means to union and life, as over against religion which seems to achieve its goals pro rata to the renunciation of the sexual act. Marriage of course gets a religious sanction, but sex is tolerated only with this sanction, and, as a value in itself, is repudiated. The Catholic Church is only quite logical when it curses anyone who will not admit that the state of virginity is superior to that of matrimony. To Philo sex was always sin except for the single purpose of begetting children. Yet for this "higher" religion many of the less crudely sexual symbols have continued. Even in ancient Egypt the more thoughtful minds developed the conception that the supreme God is hermaphroditic, reproducing himself by having within himself organs both male and female, father and mother, while the child is only an alter ego of the father. The three, father, mother and child are one. This conception was very common in the later Roman empire when it openly emerged in the Orphic hymns, and seems to lie behind not only the hermaphroditic figures of late antiquity, but also the effeminate representations of Dionysos and Apollo which fill the museums.

It is with the divine child that we, still the baby, can identify ourselves more easily than with the father's majestic greatness, and in asserting the identity of the son with the father in the divine realm, the son who is ourselves, we finally satisfy the "Oedipus," if I may use that useful but dubious term, by being ourselves one with the father in cosmic completeness.

Symbolic representation of this experience or projection or idea may depict only the child with its mother: In this the father is mysteriously implied. Sometimes we represent the three, the "holy family." On the contrary, though, in halachic Judaism the father has the kindness and brooding wings of the mother ascribed to him. Wisdom as the distinct mother breaks through so rarely as to suggest a foreign invasion of symbolism, one which halachic Judaism never really naturalised for itself. In such Judaism the devotee is still the son, and the Psalms are full of the language of childhood. But in rabbinic tradition the mystical element of identification has been repressed: the way to the father, I have said, is by obedience, a pattern which, while it alleviates the sense of guilt, still accentuates the duality of father and devotee. It is in religions centering not in obedience but in the birth and death and resurrection of the god or his son that mystical assimilation of the devotee with the father is the religious objective. For in identifying ourselves with the baby, and the baby with the father, we make ourselves one with the father. So our cycle is complete. The reality and life, as well as the protection, of baby, mother, and father are at last fully our own, and the life-urge, the "Oedipus," and the vagaries of the "id" have come into so complete a satisfaction that we see no terror even in death for this newly found masterly existence. The death of the child and his resurrection, motifs so apt to appear in the "family," are elaborations of this experience to allow even the death-urge to take us away from our guilt complexes into still more serene perfection. This was, apparently, what lay behind the movement which we call generally Orphism. Of course the new pattern of sexual realization through literal repression and spiritual approximation appealed deeply to only a minority, as religion of deep emotion appeals to only a minority in any generation. The majority are always easily content with delegating the responsibilities to others, and with the immediate ritual, such as wearing an amulet or attending stated functions and festivals. Yet it must be recalled that it is always the devout, the fanatics, who show the real meaning of the symbols of all religions, meaning which is felt by others in proportion to the emotional depth of their religious experiences. The new repressed symbols (which were rarely altogether new) of the refined Bacchism varied; but most commonly in one way or another they represented life-fluid still; and though the life-fluid no longer overtly flows from the divine phallus, it still makes one born anew as the divine person in so far as it gives immortality.

This development has been sketched here from the masculine point of view, and in patriarchal society. I do not know feminine psychology or matriarchy. It is obvious that the basic experience of the tiny infant with the mother is common to both the boy and the girl. It is also evident that the girl in her own way is as anxious to achieve unity with the father as the boy can be. But somewhere in most girls' development is a stage of transfer, so that the girl's ideal is, by possessing the father, to become herself a mother, the mother; just as the boy's aspiration is to become the father by possessing the mother. I do not think this difference need bother us. The symbols of religion in the civilizations from which we are descended seem largely to be the product of men, rather than women, though perhaps the satyr with Dionysos, and the absence of such a figure from among Astarte's followers, are results of the greater influence of women in Bacchism than among the Semites. I suspect that before a Madonna and Child the woman identifies herself as much with the mother as the man identifies himself with the child. But I am certain we can go a long way without having to stop at each step to discuss the feminine alternatives. At least I shall not attempt to do so.

From such a point of view the meaning of the symbolic *lingua franca* seemed to become much clearer. The symbols which Jews, and secondarily the Christians, had borrowed from paganism, relentlessly trace back to a common body of symbolic roots. They turn out to be used in other religions always (so far as a value can be determined for them at all) for a certain type of religious experience. Dionysiac symbols, like those of Isis, had little appeal to Romans so long as they kept to the old formal and apotropaic gods of Roman religion, though the mystic symbols of the Greek instantly appeared to the Etruscans. In Israel Yahwistic leaders had fought for centuries the conceptions and practices of the fertility cults of their neighbours: much had crept into the great Temple from these cults, as well as into the lives of Jews in general, but Yahwism finally triumphed, and with it the abolition of all that was still recognizably akin to Baal and Astarte. That is, the formal state religions, the religions which expressed themselves in stated laws and observances, such as the official religions of Athens, Rome, and Jerusalem, had quite another basis from that always implied in these symbols, and correspondingly had little use for the symbols we are studying.

The evidence, it appears, shows that these symbols were of use only in religions of deep emotion, of ecstasy, religions directly and consciously centered in the renewing of life and the granting of immortality, in the giving to the devotee a portion of the divine spirit or life-substance. Not on the forum at

Rome, they were everywhere in mystical Pompeii and ecstatic Phrygia and North Africa. Largely absent from official Athens, they were common in the popular Athens of the bases. Never in the manners and teachings of the Pharisees, they became central in Christianity for its hope of divine life here and forever.

These are the symbols which we now find in the synagogues and graves of Jews through the Roman Empire. It must be recalled again that I have been studying the symbols so intensely just because they come from the Jews of Rome, North Africa, Palestine, Dura: Jews from whom we have *no* literary survivals, and yet whose Judaism it is our desire if possible to begin to understand.

At the end of the study a type of Judaism will seem to have been indicated in which, as in Philonic Judaism, the basic idea of "mystery" had been superimposed upon Jewish legalism. The Judaism of the rabbis was essentially a path through *this* life, the Father's code of instructions as to how we may please him while we are alive. To this, the symbols seem to say, had now been added the burning desire of the Mysteries or of gnosticism to leave this life altogether, to renounce the flesh and go up into the richness of divine existence, to appropriate God's life to oneself.

The experience, it will appear, seemed to imply at times the initial destruction of one's self, life achieved through death, and it was expressed in pagan hunting scenes, in the god Dionysos the hunted hunter, in the rabbit, deer, or bull torn by other animals, in the all-devouring lion's mask; it was the basis for all mystic interpretation (of whatever antiquity) of the sacrificial system of pagans and Jews. In Christianity the idea persisted in the Lamb who was slain and in whose death we also die, that we may rise in his resurrection. With no suggestion that in Judaism the animal torn had such a specific reference as did the Lamb to Jesus in Christianity, the religious pattern seems basically identical.

Or the experience could be represented in the apposite terms, terms of victory in the mystic ἀγών or conflict, the spiritualization of the wars and religious games of Greece, and even of her cock fights; for the afflatus of victory in these corresponded with amazing accuracy to the afflatus of religious achievement. When religion has brought one into such a richness of life and love that even death is defeated, the tombstone may well show in triumphant symbols that Victory and her crown belong to the entombed. This crown of victory in life's ἀγών was for Philo the final Vision. For all, it meant immortality. Hence the various symbols of victory, or even Victory herself, on the Jewish synagogues and graves would seem to indicate that the Jews who used them also looked for this victory, this crown.

Or the experience could be symbolized in quite different terms, those of birth, of craving for the divine fluid, and getting it. So with the original phallic meaning entirely obscured to Christians and Jews, and largely repressed even by pagans, still all alike, pagans, Jews, and Christians, sought the cup with its medicine of immortality, the life juice of God himself, which in early times was released by the lustful satyr, but now in all three religions was made available by the endearing little erotes, the cupids, whose loving symbolism was not obscured even when they lost their wings. And for the devout of all three religions the vine was depicted holding within its folds a multitude of symbols of love, symbols of God's mercies to man, and of man's safety in God's love of man and in man's love for god.

Or the experience could be depicted in terms of the zodiac, the planets, the cosmos, with which man unites himself as he becomes the macrocosmos, or as he is carried by the solar eagle to the top of the universe, if not outside it altogether to that Sun and Ideal World of which the material sun and universe are only imperfect copies.

Or the old fertility identification could survive in the Seasons, depicted on synagogue and grave with their fruits, to represent the great cycle of death and resurrection in nature, the cycle in which man first, perhaps, saw definite promise of his own immortality.

These ideas have as little place in normative, rabbinic Judaism as do the pictures and symbols and gods which Jews borrowed to suggest them. That such ideas could have been borrowed by Jews was no surprise to me after years of studying Philo, for in him I had long known intimately a man who had thought such ideas to be the deepest meaning of the Jewish Torah itself. Such conceptions in Judaism will be no surprise, either, to students of Cabbala. What will be perplexing is to know how Jews fitted such conceptions into, or harmonised them with, the Bible. For it is obvious that no religion could have borrowed the group of mystic ideas which I have suggested are implied in the symbols, without harmonising them in some way with their own myths, or their own myths with the mystic ideas. Otherwise the borrowing would mean an actual abandonment of the old religion and taking on of a new one. Jewish explanations must have been given to the old pagan symbols and their values if the devotees, as they patently did, remained Jews. We have a vivid example of that process when Plutarch interprets the myths of Isis to harmonise them with the mystical Platonism of his day. Plutarch shows also how Dionysiac myths had previously been retold to adapt them to the same mystical philosophy. In both Philo and the Cabbala the method of assimilating mystic aspiration with the Torah was that of allegory, though the elaborate numerical allegory of Hebrew words by Cabbalists, gamatria, was of course different from Philo's allegory. In the complete absence of writings by Jews who used the symbols, the O.T. paintings of Dura are accordingly of prime importance. For, in a setting of the pagan symbols, the Dura synagogue presents a pageant of Old Testament scenes completely allegorized: they are in no case simple illustrations of Old Testament scenes or passages. From them we can catch actual glimpses of the integration of Old Testament story with mystic hope in this later and otherwise unknown stage of hellenistic Judaism. To demonstrate this is the final task of my study.

In the centuries after the fall of Jerusalem, when Jews were without a national center or, in their loss of both Hebrew and Aramaic, a single unifying language, and when there was no Talmud to control their interpretations of the Old Testament, or of the Law, it seems the most natural thing in the world that such Jews should thus have accepted the mysticism of Hellenism, and fused it with their Jewish traditions. That the Jews survived as a group at all is the great miracle, and was possible, even as miracle, only as they kept their sense of distinction constantly vivid by observing the practices of the Law, especially by marrying for the most part within the group, and by holding their Torah in utter uniqueness. But there was nothing to keep them from being otherwise hellenized, gnosticized, and attracted by the philosophy of the late Roman World. How far the Jews went at that time in adopting the gentile idea that religion, and especially their own religion, is a mystic source of life for this and for the next world, we have no way of knowing. Probably, as in Philo's day, there was no unanimity, and some Jews were almost complete gnostics and laid the foundations of later Caballism, while others were of what Philo called the "literalist" type; they were content, that is, simply to obey the precepts. The most difficult point of all to believe is the point about which there can be no dispute whatever, that they could have been so hellenised as to borrow for their amulets, charms, graves, and synagogues the mystic art symbols of paganism, even the forms of some of the gods themselves. For no error of induction or fancy in my own thinking can obscure the fact that Jews did borrow this art, not sporadically but for their most sacred and official associations. This I did not invent, and now no competent historian of the field may ignore or slight it.

Chapter Nine

The Rabbis and Jewish Art in the Greco-Roman Period[1]

Hebrew Union College Annual 1961, 32:269-279

A person who presents a novel thesis in the humanities must expect a good deal of misunderstanding. The chief difficulty, indeed, is to keep one's fellow scholars within the limits proposed, since they so often reject the suggestion in a form they have exaggerated beyond anything originally set forth. Over thirty years ago I said that Philo's interpretation of Jewish laws suggested that the Jewish law courts of Alexandria were making many decisions which adjusted Jewish traditions to those in force in Roman Alexandria. My suggestion, so far as I know, is now generally accepted. At the time several scholars thought it invalid because later rabbis could be shown to have made similar adjustments in a few details, from which it was at once concluded that all Alexandrian decisions must have reflected the jurisprudence of the courts in first century Palestine. Such a nonsequitur is no longer urged.

In my *By Light, Light,* I pointed out how drenched in the language of pagan mystery religions is Philo's interpretation of the religious values of the Torah, and how it seemed to me possible, indeed likely, that some Jews in Alexandria, at least, carried out their Sabbath and Festival cultus with a feeling that in contrast to pagans, Jews had the true rites which brought mystic rewards. Again my thesis was exaggerated by others to make me mean that Philo's mystic language could not have corresponded to any reality, unless Judaism in Alexandria had been completely changed by the introduction of formal ceremonies of initiation, cult dramas, and the like. Nothing disproves such a thesis, but there was not evidence for it at all, as it was easy to show. The issue was presented as an absolute dilemma: either the mystery language meant nothing whatever, was a mere *façon de parler,* or the Jews meant by it the full machinery of the celebrations of Isis or Eleusis. It has taken a number of years for my actual thesis to be considered on its merits, and now be widely accepted.

---

[1]No one could better exemplify the thesis of this paper, and of most of my studies, than Dr. Julian Morgenstern. His life has demonstrated how deeply one can preserve the best in rabbinic Judaism while disagreeing with much in the teaching of the rabbis; and how one can appropriate the soul of Gentile thought and scholarship and still live dedicated to the People and their God.

To feel mystic value in the Kiddush or Seder is something mystic Jews have always done. Jews who read mystic values into the word of the Torah, as did not only Philo's group but also followers of Merkavah and all mystic Jews to the Hasidim could hardly be expected to stop such "nonsense," as many halachic rabbis considered it, when they lifted the cup or blessed the bread. Nor did they.

Now after the increasing acceptance of my real thesis on mystic Judaism I have aroused fresh protest by suggesting that the archeological discoveries from Greco-Roman Jewry must be taken seriously as the only evidence we have from that group as a whole. Actually, the various archeologists who discovered the data could hardly believe their eyes, and it was not until I had published the first three volumes of my *Jewish Symbols* in 1953 that more than a small fraction of the learned world had any conception of the nature and extent of this material. The objects seems to violate all the traditions of orthodox Judaism. The more one studied them, the more one saw that they could not be brushed aside as ornament, as some tried to do, after the analogy of the designs of the seventeenth and eighteenth century Jewish tombstones of Poland, or the cupids on marriage contracts of that same period. For, although many of the forms borrowed by Jews were the same in both periods, the Greco-Roman Jews were borrowing live forms from pagan religious life, in contrast to the largely ornamental cupids later Jews borrowed from baroque and rococo art. Jews of the later period did not put figures of Mary and Jesus, or the crucifix, on their tombs, or anywhere else, for these represented the living religion of the gentiles about them. But Jews in the ancient world were using the living symbols of pagans of the day, not only in synagogues, but, at Dura, elaborately integrated with biblical scenes. In graves the symbols appear with the *menorah, shofar, lulav,* and Torah shrine of Jewish worship. Certainly nothing in rabbinical tradition had given us reason to expect such combinations: as that Moses would led the Israelites from Egypt brandishing the club of Hercules; that he should be found in his basket in the Nile by the naked Aphrodite-Anahita and given to the three Nymphs to be nursed like other divine, or human-divine, babies. Rabbinic tradition had not prepared us for the goddess of Victory holding out her wreath atop the Jewish Temple; or for the cosmic bull with Gayomart and Armaiti of Iranian tradition on the temple entrance; or the Ares with Victories presiding over the Exodus. When these Jews wanted to depict the futility of contemporary paganism they could do so forcibly by showing the local gods prostrate and broken before the Ark of the Covenant, after the analogy of Dagon. But it was not their purpose when they turned the figure of the local Cavalier God into a representation of Mordecai in his triumph, or in Rome put up the dolphin and trident of Neptune along with the *shofar* and *menorah* in their tombs. The rabbis certainly held David the Psalmist in high regard, but never compared him to Orpheus, or led us to expect that he would be portrayed in a synagogue as Orpheus stilling the beasts. And so forth; the full list of the preposterous is long indeed.

Since these were all living symbols for pagans, their use by Jews involves not only the problem of rabbinic attitude toward the making of images, but of Jews' making precisely *these* images, and of introducing them not only into the synagogues and graves, but into biblical narrative itself, and among the objects used in Jewish worship. Nothing suggests that the Jews of the period ever worshipped the dolphin, any more than they worshipped the *menorah* or *shofar*. But we may assume that Jews who put the *menorah* and *shofar* on the graves at least attested their Jewish loyalty thereby. What did they attest when they put the dolphin on the grave with the Jewish objects? What did they mean by giving Moses the infancy of a demi-god, the mature power of Hercules, or by giving Mordecai the form of the Cavalier God? We must answer these questions, and all the questions raised by the other forms Jews borrowed, in one of two ways. First, we may assume that, by the fact they were Jewish, the Jews could not have meant anything at all by them, can ignore the implications of the objects represented, and simply look for gaps in the wall which the rabbis in general erected against image making and decoration. If, by this, we can show that any rabbis under any circumstances allowed any images at all, we may assume that all rabbis allowed all kinds of images everywhere, and so may see in these Jews a part of the unbroken succession of a changeless and monolithic Judaism, normative Judaism.

Although many scholars have taken substantially this line of argument, I protest that it is utterly fallacious. Basically it does not at all consider the evidence itself, the actual images and forms which these Jews made. We cannot hope to explain why the painters at Dura gave Moses the prerogatives of the divine babies, and the power of Hercules, by looking through rabbinic comments. And no amount of indignation can obscure the fact that the Jews did do this, and much else like it.

The second approach is to begin precisely with this new evidence, aware that new evidence may tell new things, do so with the a priori assumption that since Jews made the paintings, mosaics, and carvings, they might have been saying something for their Judaism which we should not have heard in the aniconic tradition of the rabbis. In reading Philo we have long had to discuss Jewish remains with such an a priori assumption about his borrowing hellenistic terms of philosophy and mystery. For we know that Hellenism profoundly affected the tone of Philo's interpretations of Judaism, to the point that the rabbis had no interest in him: we should never have heard his name if Christians had not preserved his writings. Wolfson may be right that Philo represents "native Judaism" with a Greek veneer, native Judaism which registered in his deep loyalty to the Torah, written and in practice. I have never liked Wolfson's figure of "veneer," since the Greek elements in Philo's writings do not obscure his passionate devotion to the Jewish God, Bible, and People, which have always been basic in rabbinic tradition, while a veneer is deigned precisely to conceal the cheaper wood beneath it. The figure, actually, does not represent Wolfson's own conception of Philo, and I agree with him heartily that we cannot understand Philo simply from the hellenistic schools of philosophy. Philo mingled with these a passionate commitment to Jewish tradition, as direct revelation, and, as Wolfson says, thereby represents in the history of western thought a great transition which reached its highest point in the Schoolmen. Still, I repeat, the end result in Philo himself made him so different from the rabbis that they did not like him. Living in Greco-Roman civilization could profoundly affect one's Judaism. We know that another Jew rewrote the Sibylline Books to put Moses into them, also something the rabbis did not like; and that the fragments from Alexander Polyhistor found in Eusebius show a variety of other deep modifications of "normative" Jewish attitudes on the part of individual Jews. It is well recognized that to understand these writers we must begin with their texts to see what they actually say before we judge their conformities to, or departures from, traditional Judaism; I cannot understand how there can be any question that we must do the same with archeological data. We first must discover what these Jews actually did before we consider their relation to the Judaism preserved in rabbinical writings.

What the forms themselves tell us is too elaborate a matter to rehearse in a few pages. Their relation to rabbinical tradition still remains an important problem. Rabbinic allusion to each or any of the symbols, as I shall call them for short, whether allusion in literary figures or in what rabbis say of them directly, has the greatest importance. Of many of the symbols I have discussed, however, I could find no trace in rabbinical tradition. Trained rabbinical scholars will in time find passages which I overlooked, so that in details my conclusions about different symbols can be corrected or amplified. Some symbols the rabbis did mention directly, such as the fish, bread and wine, or the eagle. Josephus and the rabbis certainly did not prepare us to find that the hated eagle was one of the most common ornaments on Galilean synagogues. That is, rabbinical mention may make the use of certain symbols in synagogues and Jewish graves more astonishing rather than less.

This is one of the many "facts" which several scholars who resist my conclusions do not discuss,[2] scholars who assume that *qua* Jewish, the archeological data must represent an acceptable and accepted part of rabbinical Judaism. The hypothesis on which I am proceeding is that the later rabbinical tradition has always correctly interpreted the Tannaim and Amoraim as deeply disliking figured representation, and allowing their use only in exceptional instances, if at all. If that is so, and yet we see that Jews of their own day commonly made such representations, then we cannot take without scrutiny the claim that those who made them were under strict rabbinic guidance and control. We ask, first, how reliable the tradition was that the rabbinical centers really did supervise world Judaism at this time; second, what the rabbis actually are

---

[2]As, for example, Ephraim E. Urbach, "The Rabbinical Law of Idolatry," *Israel Exploration Journal,* IX (1959), 149-65, 229-45.

recorded to have said about figured representations; third, what the Jews actually represented.

On the first of these there is no point in rehearsing the evidence here, since, so far as I know, the statements were adequately collected in the first chapter of Volume IV, and have often been discussed elsewhere.[3] The few allusions to the authority of the Patriarchs and Sages, or the Roman recognition of the Patriarch as Ethnarch, with "power like the kings of the Gentiles even to carrying out capital punishment," as Origen tells us, tell us nothing specific about actual authority. We must see evidence of the exercise of power before mere legends or declarations of it mean anything. Frey[4] has covered the ground excellently. The only trace that the Patriarch exercised power outside Palestine is an inscription from Stobi of the year A.D. 165, which demands that if anyone wanted to make alterations in the synagogue there he must pay the "patriarch" 25,000 dinars. But this can by no means be taken *ohne weiteres* to be the Patriarch in Palestine mentioned by Origen a century and a half later. As Frey points out, it is highly unlikely that in the desperate years of the mid-second century a Jewish official in Palestine controlled the Jews in Macedonia. We have no trace of the rabbis controlling Jewish thinking or observance outside Jewish academies. This does not prove that they had no control, but it remains that our only test of rabbinic control over the centers which produced the art is the way in which that art squares with the major rabbinic traditions and positions. I suggested that the conformity of Jewish art to rabbinic traditions up to about the mid-second century of the common era made it a likely hypothesis that the rabbis, or pre-rabbinic Sages, who hated imagery were leading popular Jewish attitudes at the time. But in the Jewish art of the next three centuries there is not a single reservation of even the most liberal Sages not flouted in the actual representations, and the general position of the *'Avodah Zarah, Mishnah* and *Gemara'*, as well as of the tannaitic Midrashim, patently rejects such representations with horror.

Here is the second point, the problem of what the rabbis of that time actually did say, or preserved from earlier rabbis, about images. On this I feel Rabbi Boaz Cohen is my best guide.[5] After a brief survey of the pre-Exilic

---

[3]From the extensive bibliography the following are a few of the more important titles: E. Schürer, *A History of the Jewish People in the Time of Jesus Christ,* 1890, II, i, 173, where the important text of Origen on the subject is quoted; G. F. Moore, *Judaism,* 1927, I, 234, III, 635 f.; J. B. Frey, *Corpus Inscriptionum Judaicarum,* 1936, pp. cx f.

[4]Frey, *op. cit.,* 504-507, inscription 694. He gives an excellent bibliography of the inscription, to which add A. Marmorstein in *Jewish Quarterly Review,* XXVII (1936/37), 373-84.

[5]"Art in Jewish Law," *Judaism,* III (1954), 165-76. He has here outlined only the basic principles, and a note says he plans a larger annotated work on the subject. This article was published simultaneously with my review of the subject in *Symbols,* IV, 3-24.

attitudes, a highly complex matter which does not affect our problem, he points out how under the Second Commonwealth, the crisis of Hellenisation produced a greater vigor in the law, so that the Mosaic prohibition of images was extended to include every animate being. That the attitude was not uniform seems suggested by the story of the eagle on Herod's temple,[6] but in general Cohen's conclusion is quite similar to that I had reached for this period.

In the tannaitic period, the first two Christian centuries, the decisions of the rabbis remained very strict. Cohen's summary of their declarations follows:

> One may not make any image in relief or in the round, be it carved out of stone, wood, or any metal, of the heaven itself, or of the heavenly servants such as angels, ministering angels, *Cherubim, Seraphim, Ofanim, Hasmalim* and *Hayyot ha-Kodesh* (the winged creatures of the heavenly chariot); or of the heavenly bodies, such as the sun, moon, stars, and the constellations *(Mazzalot);* the earth itself, as well as the mountains and the hills, seas and rivers, of any living things on earth, such as birds, beasts, creeping things, snakes, scorpions, and ferocious animals; of living things in the water, such as fish, sea-monsters, dolphins, sea worms, sea snakes *(Shabririn),* reflected images of things in the sea *(Babuah).* (Perhaps there is an allusion here to the shadow sketches known as *en skiographiois.)* Similarly the things beneath the earth, such as the abyss, the darkness, and thick darkness are forbidden.

> The Tannaim further excluded the making of images even for the purpose of ornament and beauty, as the Gentiles did in the Provinces.

The Tannaim even went on to interpret "Turn not to the idols" to mean that one should not so much as look at an image, even the image of a Roman official on a coin, though, I may say, everyone knew that no cultus was offered to an image on a coin. A signet ring could be used if it had no image of an idol, that is, a god to whom worship was paid, but could be used if the image was what Cohen translates as "an ordinary figure." Even such a figure could be worn only if it was represented in intaglio. One rabbi said that in Jerusalem many such representations could be found, but no human faces. The rabbis changed the law so as to make it possible for a Jew to live in a gentile city filled with cult images, and even for a Jew to practise the arts of sculpture and design, so long as the images Jews made were sold to gentiles. One or another of the Tannaim specified images which he considered it dangerous for a Jew to make at all: an image bearing in its hand a staff, bird, or sphere, a sword, a crown, or a ring. One can deal with a torso when found, they said, but not with an independent hand or foot, or the sun or moon, and not a dragon or a human face. Yet practically all of these are to be found in extant Jewish art, not fragments found and sold, but made directly for graves and places of Jewish worship.

---

[6] I discussed this in *Symbols,* VIII, 123-25.

The principle in all this, as it seems to me, is the close following of the Second Commandment, which had been given in two distinct parts. The first forbade making "unto thee" any graven image, etc., by which the law does not literally forbid Jews to make for gentiles, but only that Jews make images for Jews. This distinction seems to lie behind all the rabbinic pronouncements. The second part of the Commandment forbade one to worship such images once made, whether, as the rabbis correctly interpreted, made by a Jew or gentile.

Almost all of this could be repeated for the Amoraim, but Cohen rightly says that "when paintings became the regular feature of synagogue decoration of the time, the rabbis tactfully and tacitly bowed before the facts." (Actually, the sculptures of the Galilean synagogues of Capernaum and Chorazin have been dated confidently by the archeologists in the last years of the Tannaim.) Cohen concludes that the Amoraim: 1) took no exception to mosaics in the synagogues; 2) allowed sculpture of all living beings except, in combination, of the four living beings of the Heavenly Chariot; 3) continued to forbid a ring with a human figure on it in relief; 4) always forbade engravings of human figures as well as sculpture of angels and heavenly bodies. Cohen takes it to represent the opinion of the Amoraim in general when a single rabbi, or a pair of rabbis, relaxes slightly to allow paintings and mosaics, "bowed before the facts." Actually the record of their bowing may well, as so often, simply have recorded a minority opinion. Granted that Cohen is entirely right, however, such bowing by no means explains what prompted Jews in the first place to make the great change. For it was indeed a great change when they began commonly to produce not only paintings, but mosaics and carvings in deep relief, in which they represented the human figure, Helios, Dionysus, centaurs, eagles, and the like, began to make them in the tannaitic period.

So we find ourselves involved in the third aspect of the problem. We must ask what were the "facts" before which the rabbis bowed, or, as Urbach puts it, "the reality with which the Sages had to reckon even if they did not approve of it." To Urbach, the "reality" is the problem of Jews' living in idolatrous cities, and making their living by manufacturing objects for gentiles to use in idol worship. Cohen sees much more clearly that for us the more important fact before which the rabbis had to bow was that Jews were making the forbidden forms "for themselves," forms which they used (the question is, how used) in connection with their own worship of the Jewish God. For the rabbis had to face not only the "reality" of Jews living among gentiles, but the "fact" that Jews were putting practically all the forbidden forms into their synagogues. I have all along insisted that without direct evidence to the contrary, of which not a scrap exists, we must assume that Jewish worship was never directed to these forms, not even in the symbolic sense that in bowing before the image one really bowed before the reality behind it. I have seen no evidence that Jews ever bowed before images. But the evidence is abundant that the rabbis had to bow before the presence of images in Jewish graves and synagogues.

Both of these phrases, the rabbis having to "reckon with reality," and "bow before the facts," represent my position exactly, once we have clearly in mind what were the reality and facts. There were things going on in Jewry which the rabbis "did not approve." That Jews made these forms "for themselves," and put them in their places of holiest association, violated the spirit of such Judaism as appears in Josephus and the rabbis.

The problem is not whether a few rabbis can be shown to have bowed before the situation, but what prompted Jews to introduce the forms at all. Who started such a movement, and why? Certainly not the rabbis as a group themselves. In Beth She'arim rabbis are buried in plain sarcophagi along with the sarcophagi of Jews on which were blatantly carved reliefs of the most forbidden subjects, such as that of the sun as a human face, Zeus Helios.

Another bit of evidence, by no means adequately appraised, shows that what we would call orthodox Jews had to tolerate representations they did not approve. For after the paintings were finished in the Dura synagogue some person or persons came into the building and scratched out the eyes of many of the figures in the lowest register, did it so skillfully that the desecration can be recognized only by careful scrutiny. This could hardly have been done, as Kraeling suggested, by the desperate men who wrecked the synagogue for the city's final defense of its wall, since such people, if they did not like the paintings, would presumably have shown their contempt by hitting the faces with their shovels, rather than by so meticulously picking out the eyes. A better guess at what happened lies immediately at hand. Urbach discusses the rabbinic practice of "annulling" images so that they could not be called "images" any more. He quotes the passage I had discussed in which R. El'azar bar Kappara, as he transliterates the name, beat a gentile until the gentile would desecrate or annul the image on a ring which the rabbi had found and wanted to keep. Any kind of defacement would do when a gentile did it, apparently, but when in the third century Rabbi Samuel saw his colleague, Rav Judah, wearing a ring on which a figure stood out in relief, Samuel called Judah a scornful name and ordered him specifically to "put out that fellow's eye." It would seem that some one or more Jews at Dura wanted the figures in these paintings, which seemed to them scandalous, annulled. It might possibly have been the artists themselves, to take away any grounds for accusation that they had painted objects and forms for worship; but in that case it is hard to see why only figures in the lowest register were thus treated, or why in no case is the eye damaged on a pagan divinity (Orpheus, Ares, Victory, Tyche). None of these was the lowest register. The only probable guess is that one or more Jews at Dura did not like such figures at all, thought them conducive to idolatry, and came in secretly to annul what of them could be reached by standing on the benches, did it so carefully that they would not be caught. I strongly suspect that most rabbis in the great tradition would have applauded the act, since even the more liberal rabbis, who held that all features of bird and beast might be copied, still did not allow the human countenance. The natural assumption from such evidence is that the dominant Jews at Dura liked and made the representations, or had them made, but that others in the congregation did not like them at all. Still, presumably, they tolerated one another within the same congregation. Those who scratched out the eyes clearly did not want to be caught: that is, they wanted to remain within the community. We need only look at the new state of Israel to see again Jews of all sorts, who completely disagree in their interpretation of Jewish law and worship, cooperating magnificently.

Our real question is direct and simple, however difficult to find the answer: what were the sources and inspiration of the representations we find in ancient Jewish synagogues and graves? We need not dispute whether the Jews at Dura, Randanini, Hammam Lif, Beth Alpha, and Capernaum were either "totally different" from the rabbis, or thought identically with them. Either extreme seems absurd to me. The question is whether, as we look for the incentive which demanded and produced the art, we may find it in the rabbinic tradition. I can see, at Dura for example, a few details which recall rabbinic 'Aggadah. But this by no means indicates that the artists of Dura were inspired by rabbinical ideas to make such pictures in the first place, that they must have had the stories directly from rabbis or rabbinical writings, or that all their course of thinking followed rabbinical leadings. Nothing whatever suggests that those who lived solely within the rabbinic *Denkweise* would themselves have wanted to make the paintings, or the mosaics and carvings elsewhere. A new force, a new movement in Judaism, seems to have created the new "reality," the "facts," before which the rabbis, some of them, had to bow. Since the forms themselves can be shown to have been deeply meaningful in pagan religious thinking and feeling, my "theory" is that some Jews in more direct contact with Greco-Roman civilization thought that their religion, or their lives, would be enriched by the conceptions in which these art forms had a place. They thought so with such conviction that they took the forms even into their graves and synagogues, and mingled them with their cult objects and the heroes from Holy Writ. If it is inconceivable, as it is to me, that the rabbis of whom we know would not just have tolerated, but have led such a movement, we must ask who then did lead it, and why? The personalities we shall never know (beyond names in inscriptions), but I doubt if the movement was begun by any one man. Since Jews borrowed such generally similar forms throughout the Roman world, the movement was presumably a generally popular one, somewhat analogous to the development of Reform Judaism, which had in Moses Mendelssohn rather a spokesman and organizer than an originator. The forms which Jews borrowed from pagans in antiquity suggest a movement little resembling modern Reform, except that both meant that Jews were in each case taking into their lives what seemed to them valuable from gentile civilization. For neither of them did it mean accepting the religious cultus of the gentiles; for both it meant accepting ideas which did not come from, or generally please, the halakhic rabbis. In both cases the rabbis, some of them, only "bowed to the facts."

That this was true in the modern world we know very well. That it was true in the ancient world is my hypothetical suggestion, and to it scholars must bow until they can produce a hypothesis which better explains the facts. In any case we must all, and always, bow to the facts. Since the Jewish symbols offer a new body of evidence, indeed a new kind of evidence, it will force all of us to be at least open to new conclusions. I have no illusion that in my *Symbols* I have exhausted, or pin-pointed, the ideas which Jews took from gentiles and illustrated with gentile plastic forms. We cannot determine, however, what Jews had in mind when they borrowed the gentile forms by showing that a few rabbis did not object when other Jews began to use them.

Index